TEMPO

Olivia Johnston
Chris Barker and Libby Mitchell

WORKBOOK 3

MACMILLAN

G000320729

Module	Unit		
Module 1	1 The match starts at 11	Grammar file	page 4
		Vocabulary	page 6
		Dialogue work	page 6
		Grammar practice: Present simple of *be*, revision; Present simple, revision; Present continuous, revision; Present continuous and *going to* for future, revision; Responding with *So* and *Nor*;	page 6
		Skills development	page 10
		Study tips	page 11
		Talk time	page 12
		Let's check	page 13
	2 We have to check in at 2.15	Grammar file	page 14
		Vocabulary	page 16
		Dialogue work	page 17
		Grammar practice: *must/mustn't*, revision; *have to*; Past simple of *be*, revision; Past simple of regular and irregular verbs, revision; Past continuous, revision	page 17
		Culture spot: Charles Dickens	page 20
		Portfolio	page 21
		Let's read	page 22
		Let's check	page 23
		Extra!	page 24
Module 2	3 We've had an e-mail from Tommaso	Grammar file	page 26
		Vocabulary	page 28
		Dialogue work	page 28
		Grammar practice: Present perfect simple; Present perfect with *been* and *gone*; Present perfect interrogative with *ever* + short answers	page 29
		Skills development	page 32
		Study tips	page 33
		Talk time	page 34
		Let's check	page 35
	4 Your wish has just come true!	Grammar file	page 36
		Vocabulary	page 38
		Dialogue work	page 39
		Grammar practice: Present perfect with *just*, *already*, *yet*, *for* and *since*	page 39
		Culture spot: School in the USA	page 42
		Portfolio	page 43
		Let's read	page 44
		Let's check	page 45
		Extra!	page 46
Module 3	5 Saturday morning on the farm	Grammar file	page 48
		Vocabulary	page 50
		Dialogue work	page 51
		Grammar practice: *if* with the Present simple and with *might*; First conditional; Question tags	page 51
		Skills development	page 54
		Study tips	page 55
		Talk time	page 56
		Let's check	page 57
	6 It's great to be outside	Grammar file	page 58
		Vocabulary	page 60
		Dialogue work	page 61
		Grammar practice: *used to* + infinitive; adjectives followed by infinitive; the infinitive of purpose; verbs followed by the *-ing* form	page 61
		Culture spot: A Cotswold Village	page 64
		Portfolio	page 65
		Let's read	page 66
		Let's check	page 67
		Extra!	page 68

Module	Unit		
Module 4	7	**The girl who lives in Mexico City**	
		Grammar file	page 70
		Vocabulary	page 72
		Dialogue work	page 72
		Grammar practice: relative pronouns: *who, which, where, whose*;	
		Present simple passive	page 73
		Skills development	page 76
		Study tips	page 77
		Talk time	page 78
		Let's check	page 79
	8	**Somebody's always late**	
		Grammar file	page 80
		Vocabulary	page 82
		Dialogue work	page 82
		Grammar Practice: pronouns beginning *some-, any-, no-, every-*;	
		reported requests and commands with *told* and *asked*;	
		Second conditional	page 83
		Culture spot: Cornwall	page 86
		Portfolio	page 87
		Let's read	page 88
		Let's check	page 89
		Extra!	page 90
Module 5	9	**I'd gone to the cinema**	
		Grammar file	page 92
		Vocabulary	page 94
		Dialogue work	page 95
		Grammar practice: Past perfect simple; reported statements with	
		say and *tell*	page 95
		Skills development	page 98
		Study tips	page 99
		Talk time	page 100
		Let's check	page 101
	10	**We've been waiting here for ages**	
		Grammar file	page 102
		Vocabulary	page 104
		Dialogue work	page 104
		Grammar practice: Present perfect continuous; Present perfect	
		continuous with *for* and *since*; Past simple passive;	
		reported questions	page 105
		Culture spot: Fish and Chips	page 108
		Portfolio	page 109
		Let's read	page 110
		Let's check	page 111
		Extra!	page 112
	Portfolio Dossier	Write a film review	page 114
		Vocabulary builder	page 116

GRAMMAR FILE

Present simple of *be (revision)*

I am very late.
You're early.
Where is she?
He isn't hungry.
It's very cold today.
Are we ready to leave now? Yes, we are.
No, you aren't.
Are they in the garden?

- We use the short form of the verb *be* in spoken English and informal written English.
- In questions, the verb *be* comes before the subject.
- We always use the long form of the verb *be* in affirmative short answers, e.g. *Are you ready? Yes, we are.* NOT: ~~Yes, we're.~~

Present simple (revision)

I live in Brighton.
Where do you live?
Does she like sport?
Yes, she does. She plays football every Saturday.
Does Marek usually wear glasses?
No, he doesn't.
We usually go to the beach at the weekend.
Which beach do you usually go to?
They don't get up early on Saturdays.

- We use the Present simple for permanent situations and routines, e.g. *I live in Cambridge. She always walks to school.*
- We often use adverbs of frequency with the Present simple, e.g. *We often play tennis in the summer. Do you ever read comics?*
- We also use the Present simple to talk about things that generally happen, e.g. *It snows here in the winter. It doesn't rain a lot in August.*
- The Present simple affirmative has the same endings for all persons except the third person singular, which always ends in *-s.*
- We form the Present simple negative with *don't* or, in the third person singular, *doesn't.*
- We form questions in the Present simple with *do* or, in the third person singular, *does.*

Present continuous (revision)

Ssh! I'm listening to something on the radio.
Why are you wearing my sunglasses?
My sister is playing basketball at the moment.
Mr Adams isn't working today.
Your cat is watching the hamster in its cage.
We're making a chocolate cake.
What are you two drawing in your notebooks?
They're talking. They aren't doing their homework.

- We use the Present continuous for actions which are happening at the moment when we are speaking, e.g. *Ssh! I'm listening to the radio.*
- We also use it to talk about actions which are happening during the present period, e.g. *We're studying Africa in Geography at the moment.*
- We form the Present continuous with the present simple of the verb *be* + the present participle of the verb (*listening, watching, writing, running, sitting* etc).

Present continuous for the future (revision)

I'm having a party next weekend.
What are you doing on Saturday?
Samir is taking me to a football match.
Leila is arriving on Sunday.
We aren't going to the concert next week.
You're coming to our house on Monday.
Are they leaving tomorrow?

- We also use the Present continuous to talk about fixed arrangements for the future, especially when we say the time, e.g. *Nick is leaving at four thirty. Maria isn't playing in the match next week. What time are they arriving on Saturday?*

Going to for the future (revision)

I'm going to learn Spanish next year.
Are you going to tell your parents?
Who is going to help?
It isn't going to rain.
We're going to win this match.
You're going to lose.
What are they going to say about the mess?

- We use *going to* to talk about a planned future action, e.g. *I'm going to learn to skate this year.*
- We also use it to talk about something we can predict because of what is happening now, e.g. *Look at those clouds. It's going to rain.*
- The future with *going to* is formed with the Present continuous of *go + to +* the base form of the verb, e.g. *I am going to buy a guitar.*

Agreeing with affirmative statements

So am/are/is ...
I'm staying in bed today. So am I.
You're late. So are you.
Liza's playing well. So is Nina.
My parents are getting up early tomorrow. So are mine.

So do/does ...
I love swimming. So do I.
You eat a lot of sweets. So do you.
Finn wants to be an actor. So does Andy.
Jo and Ella live near the school. So do Ryan and Kath.

- We use *So am/is/are* and *So do/does* to agree with affirmative ideas, e.g. *'We're going to Spain this summer.' 'So are we.'* (= We are going to Spain, too.) *'My brother plays the guitar.' 'So does mine.'* (= My brother plays the guitar too.)

Agreeing with negative statements

Nor am/are/is.....
I'm not thirsty. Nor am I.
You aren't ready. Nor are you.
Rose isn't in the team. Nor is Veronica.
Suzy and Fran aren't coming. Nor are Jack and Adam.

- We use *Nor am/is/are* and *Nor do/does* to agree with negative ideas, e.g. *'My mother isn't in a very good mood.' 'Nor is mine.' 'I don't drink coffee.' 'Nor do I.'*

Nor do/does ...
I don't like golf. Nor do I.
You don't know the answer. Nor do you.
Tim doesn't listen in class. Nor does Ryan.
My parents don't drive to work. Nor do mine.

- We can use *Neither* instead of *Nor*. They mean exactly the same, e.g. *'I'm not sporty.' 'Neither am I.'* OR: *'Nor am I.'*
'You don't get up early.' 'Neither do you.' OR: *'Nor do you.'*

The match starts at 11

Vocabulary

1 **Make a word from Box A with a word from Box B and label the pictures of sports kit.**

BOX A	BOX B
baseball	skirt
cycling	shorts
~~football~~	shirt
golf	goggles
rugby	costume
skiing	~~club~~
swimming	~~boots~~
tennis	bat

1 football boots..........   2 ....

3 ....   4 ....

 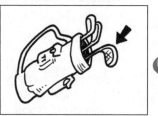

5 ....   6 ....

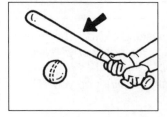 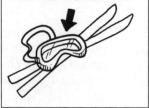

7 ....   8 ....

Dialogue work

2 **Complete the dialogue with the correct sentences.**

Becky Sit down, Eddie.

Eddie (1) ..Why?..

Becky You're standing in front of the TV and I can't see it.

Eddie (2) ....

Becky It's an American programme called *The Team*.

Eddie (3) ....

Becky I try to. But some of my friends don't let me.

Eddie (4) ....
....

Becky Well, sometimes my friends stand in front of the TV and talk.

Eddie (5) ....

Becky Er … so do I, Eddie. Now can you please sit down and be quiet?

Eddie (6) ....
....

Becky Good.

- Sorry. I'm not going to say another word.
- ~~Why?~~
- What do you mean? Who doesn't let you?
- What are you watching?
- I hate people like that.
- Do you watch it every week?

Grammar practice

3 **Complete the sentences with the present tense of the verb *be*.**

'...Are... you ready?' 'Yes, we ...are...'

1 Football .... my favourite sport.

2 '........... you in the tennis team?' 'No, we ....'

3 Why .... he always late?

4 There's a pool near my house but there .... a tennis court.

5 I .... very good at sport. I don't like getting hot and tired!

6 These .... my goggles. They're yours.

4 Write sentences in the Present simple using the correct verb from the list.

> play   do   go

How often / you / football?
How often do you play football?

1 your sister / athletics?

....

2 They / baseball in the USA

....

3 Ellie / not / a lot of sport because she hates it!

....

....

4 your sisters / riding in the park?

....

....

5 Which day / you and Joey / gymnastics?

....

....

6 you / sometimes / volleyball on the beach?

....

....

5 Match the sentences and responses. Then write them in the Present continuous.

Ssh! I (watch) the big match on TV.
Ssh! I'm watching the big match on TV.
Who's playing? .... [d]

1 (you feel) OK?

....

.... [ ]

2 (Eddie eat) again?

....

....

.... [ ]

3 (we /win)?

....

....

.... [ ]

4 Zoe (not play) very well.

....

.... [ ]

5 What (Adam do)?

....

....

.... [ ]

a) He (run) towards the goal.
b) No, we (lose), I'm afraid.
c) She (do) her best.
d) ~~Who (play)?~~
e) Yes, he (have) his third ham sandwich!
f) Yes, I (feel) better now.

6 Use the diary to write Kirsty's plans for next week in the Present continuous.

Monday
Gymnastics with Sonia. Then have lunch together.
1 Tuesday
Tennis with Rosie. Meet her at the tennis club.
2 Wednesday
Stay at home. Help Mum with the housework.
3 Thursday
Get up early. Collect Katie from the airport.
4 Friday
Athletics. Spend the whole day at the school track.

On Monday I'm doing gymnastics with Sonia.
Then we're having lunch together.

1 ....

....

....

2 ....

....

....

3 ....

....

....

4 ....

....

....

7 **Complete the sentences with a verb from the list in the Present continuous. Then write P (present) or F (future) next to each sentence.**

carry	~~look at~~	run	visit	wear
hold	read	stay	watch	

Why ...are..... you ....looking at..... me like that?
Are you angry? [P]

1 .... you .... in the
   800 metre race or the 500 metres this afternoon?
   [ ]

2 Please be quiet. I .... a really
   exciting story. [ ]

3 We .... n't .... at
   a hotel next weekend. We're camping. [ ]

4 We .... my cousins in
   Bristol next weekend. [ ]

5 I .... not .... your
   bag for you tomorrow. [ ]

6 .... you .... *The
   Simpsons* on TV this evening? [ ]

7 Why .... you ....
   my socks like that? Do they smell? [ ]

8 That's Dave. He .... a blue
   tracksuit. [ ]

8 **Respond to these statements using
So ... and Nor ... .**

I'm always late for my dance class.
..So am............ I.

My parents don't like rap music.
.Nor do........... mine.

1 We're going to the beach at the weekend.
   .... I.

2 I don't know any good shoe shops.
   .... I.

3 Your socks are really dirty.
   .... yours.

4 I don't eat meat.
   .... we.

5 Sandra's really good at languages.
   .... you.

6 My dog loves his food.
   .... my cat.

7 I'm carrying two bags.
   .... Freddie.

8 You aren't helping.
   .... Max.

9 Maria always talks in the cinema.
   .... you.

10 We aren't running in the next race.
   .... I.

11 You aren't ready yet.
   .... you.

12 Jade never dances at parties.
   .... Finn.

9 **Circle the correct form, and write PC
(Present continuous) or PS (Present
simple) in the box.**

Be quiet! Who (*makes /* (*is making*)) that horrible
noise?   [PC]

1 We often (*go / are going*) for picnics on the
   beach in the summer.   [ ]

2 'What's that music?' 'My mother (*plays / is
   playing*) one of her strange CDs!'   [ ]

3 (*Do you wear / Are you wearing*) a uniform at
   your school?   [ ]

4 You (*don't wear / aren't wearing*) your glasses
   today.   [ ]

5 What (*do you do / are you doing*) with that bag
   of sweets?   [ ]

6 We never (*go / are going*) swimming in the
   winter. The water's too cold.   [ ]

7 Sometimes we (*win / are winning*), but not
   always.   [ ]

8 Be careful! You (*stand / are standing*) on my
   jacket.   [ ]

10 Put the verbs in the Present simple or the Present continuous.

How often ....*do you go*.... (you go) swimming?

Look! John ...*is running*..... (run) across the pitch.

1 What ....……....... (you do) with my shoes?

2 What time ....…......…............ (you get up) on Saturdays?

3 Excuse me, I ....…................ (look for) the library.

4 Liam ....…......…............ (do) sport three times a week.

5 At the moment we .... (study) volcanoes in Geography.

6 My father ....….......…....... (run) four kilometres every day.

7 Why ....…...…..........…....…........ (you carry) those chairs into the garden?

8 In this photo Tara .... (wear) her grandmother's hat.

11 What are their New Year resolutions? Complete the sentences using *going to* and the correct phrases. Then write another sentence with *going to* for each picture.

In Britain people often make 'New Year resolutions' on December 31st. They decide to change their life in some way, for example, always finish their weekend homework by Friday evening.

- work out every day
- read lots of books

- save up for a camera
- ~~go for a walk every day~~

- be kind to my brother
- learn another language

31st December

1

Next year I am going to go for a walk every day. I'm going to take Thomas with me.

....

2

....
....
....
....

3

....
....
....
....

4

....
....
....
....

5

....
....
....
....

6

....
....
....
....

Sporting ambitions

Mark Todd's ambition is to be a professional tennis player. 'Tennis is the most important thing in my life,' he says. 'I want to play tennis at Wimbledon one day.'

Fourteen-year-old Mark goes to Springfield School in Brighton. [b] He's a good student and he's doing well at school, but for Mark life begins after school. At four o'clock, (**1**) [...], he cycles to his tennis club and plays tennis for two hours. His **coach**, Adrian Forester, is **pleased** with Mark's **progress**. '(**2**) [...] He's playing excellent tennis this year. And, in my opinion, he's got the right **character** to be a tennis **champion**. When he makes a **mistake**, he doesn't **lose** his head. He doesn't get upset and (**3**) [...] He's very **controlled**.'

Mark watches a lot of tennis videos. '(**4**) [...],' he says. 'I love watching Andy Roddick and Roger Federer. They're two of the best players at the moment.' He also loves watching **live** tennis matches. 'We're going to go to the Men's Finals at Wimbledon this year.

(**5**) [...]. I can't wait. The **atmosphere** at Wimbledon is really **exciting**.'

Mark's other passion in life is photography. 'I've got a **digital** camera. It's fantastic. You don't need to put a film in the camera. I take photos and **download** them onto my dad's computer. Then I **keep** the good pictures and **delete** the bad ones. At the moment I'm taking a lot of pictures of people – (**6**) [...]. It's interesting. I like watching people.'

Read

1 **Read the magazine article. Where should these sentences go?**

a) he doesn't get angry.

b) ~~His favourite subjects are English and Maths.~~

c) I learn a lot from them

d) in the park, in the street, on the bus.

e) Mark is doing very well.

f) My dad's got tickets.

g) when school finishes

2 **Read the text again and write down the meaning of these words and phrases. If you don't know them, guess and then check in a dictionary or with your teacher.**

coach ....

pleased ....

progress ....

character ....

champion ....

mistake ....

lose ....

controlled ....

live ....

atmosphere ....

exciting ....

digital ....

download ....

keep ....

delete ....

Study tips

3 **When you look words up in the dictionary, it is useful to know what kind of words they are. Look at the words in Exercise 2 again and write N (noun), V (verb) or Adj (adjective). For example: coach – N, pleased – Adj.**

Write

4 **Write about someone in your class who already knows what she/he wants to be one day. Use these sentences to help you.**

....'s ambition is to be a

.... '................................

is the most important thing in my life,' he/she says.

'I want to ....

one day.' ....-year-old

.... goes to

.... School in

.... His/Her favourite

subjects are .... and

.... She/He's a good

student and she/he's doing well at school. He/She

also enjoys ....

and ....

When he/she leaves school, he/she is going to

....

Then she/he hopes to ....

....

Talk time

1 **Write the phrases in the correct balloon.**

- Well played!
- Good luck!
- Shut up!
- Well done!
- See you there.

3 ....

Are you going to Lily's Hallowe'en party?

Yes. **1** ....
....

4 ....

2 ....

5 ....

Let's check

Vocabulary check

1 Complete the sentences with *go, do* or *play* and a sports location word.

Let's .go. to the horse races. There's a .racecourse... near my house.

1 Do you want to .... gymnastics? There's a good class at the .... in Station Road.

2 Let's .... tennis after lunch. There's a .... in the park.

3 We're going to .... football on the .... outside Dan's house.

4 I can't .... athletics at the moment because the .... is closed.

5 Let's .... swimming. There's a new .... in Market Street.

3 Circle the correct words for each sentence.

'I do a lot of sport.' 'So ... '

A I do   **B** am I   **C** do I

1 'They aren't going to have a drink.' 'Nor …'

A am I   **B** I am   **C** do I

2 … you meeting them at six?

A Do   **B** Will   **C** Are

3 'Rose doesn't eat meat.' ' … Tom.'

A So does   **B** Nor does   **C** Nor is

4 I … tennis every day next week.

A playing   **B** play   **C** am going to play

5 'Jack is very musical.' '…you.'

A Nor are   **B** So are   **C** So do

Grammar check

2 Correct the mistake in each sentence.
∧ = there's a word missing; **X** = change one word; ↳ = change the order of two words; ***** = you must delete one word.

What you looking at? ∧

What are you looking at?.......................................

1 I go usually swimming on Sundays. ↳

....

....

2 Are you going buy the new Shakira CD? ∧

....

....

3 My sister does not playing in the match on Saturday. **X** ....

....

4 You always are late for football practice. ↳

....

5 I don't like rugby and so nor does Luke. *****

....

6 I haven't got any money. How am I … home?

A getting   **B** going to get   **C** get

7 'My brother loves motorbikes.' ' … mine.'

A So is   **B** Nor does   **C** So does

8 What … to the party?

A you wear   **B** do you wear   **C** are you wearing

9 'My racket isn't here.' ' … mine.'

A Nor are   **B** So is   **C** Nor is

10 Come on! We're … the bus.

A missing   **B** going to miss   **C** to miss

GRAMMAR FILE

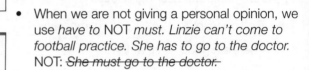

must (revision)

Affirmative

I must write to Lucy today.
You must ask Mrs Cameron.
She must do it today.
We must be careful.
They must wear warm clothes.

Negative

I mustn't make a mess.
You mustn't tell anyone.
He mustn't eat all the biscuits.
We mustn't make a noise.
They mustn't be late.

Questions

Must I wear a tie?
Must you leave now?
When must she be back?
Must we do all the exercises?
What must they do first?

- We use *must* to say that something is necessary, when we are giving our opinion, e.g. *We must be at the station by eight. Our train leaves at quarter past eight.*

- When we are not giving a personal opinion, we use *have to* NOT *must*. *Linzie can't come to football practice. She has to go to the doctor.* NOT: *She must go to the doctor.*

- We use *must not* or *mustn't* to say that something is forbidden or the wrong thing to do, e.g. *You mustn't play football in the house. You'll break something.*

- There is no past form of *must*.

have to

Affirmative

I / you / we / they have to do homework every day.
He / She has to do homework every day.

Negative

I / you / we / they don't have to wear school uniform.
He / She doesn't have to wear school uniform.

Questions

Do I / you / we / they have to bring a packed lunch?
What do I / you / we / they have to bring?
Does he / she have to bring a packed lunch?
What does he /she have to bring?

Short answers
Affirmative

Yes, I / you / we / they do.
Yes, he / she / it does.

Negative

No, I / you / we / they don't.
No, he / she / it doesn't.

- We can always use *have to* instead of *must* in the affirmative, to say that something is necessary, e.g. *We have to be at the station by eight. Our train leaves at quarter past eight.*

- The negative of *have/has to* is *don't/doesn't have to*. It does NOT have the same meaning as *mustn't*. It means that something isn't necessary, e.g. *I don't have to get up early tomorrow. It's a holiday.*

- The Past simple of *have to* is *had to*, e.g. *I didn't go to the beach because I had to do my homework.*

Past simple of *be* (revision)

I was late yesterday.
You were angry.
Where was he at ten o'clock?
He wasn't at school.
It was very hot last summer.
We weren't in London last week. Nor were we.
Were they at the rehearsal on Saturday?
No, they weren't.

- We often use the Past simple with time phrases like *yesterday, last week, last year, two weeks ago*, e.g. *I was ill last week. There weren't many people at the party on Saturday. Did you play tennis yesterday? My cousins left on Tuesday.*

Past simple of regular and irregular verbs (revision)

Regular verbs

I played tennis last week.
Did you visit Annette last night?
No, I didn't. I stayed in and watched TV.
My sister visited her friend.
We didn't enjoy the film yesterday. Nor did we.
Which film did you see?
Did they talk about the holidays?
Yes, they did. And they also talked about the match.

Irregular verbs

I went home early yesterday.
What time did you get up this morning?
Sue didn't go out at the weekend. Nor did Mark.
What did you give Carol for her birthday?
We gave her a CD.
Did you see her yesterday? Yes, we did.
Did Joey and Alice make a cake?
No, they didn't. But they bought one.

- Regular verbs in the Past simple affirmative always end in *-ed.*
- A lot of very common verbs have an irregular affirmative form in the Past simple. There are no rules for how to form them. You just have to learn them by heart! There's a list of irregular verbs on page 135 of the Student's Book.
- To make a negative statement in the Past simple, we use *didn't* + the base form, e.g. *I didn't stay with my cousins last week. They didn't go out last night.*
- To make a question in the Past simple, we use *did* + the base form, e.g. *Did you watch the match? When did they leave?*

Past continuous (revision)

I was watching TV at five o'clock yesterday.
What were you doing?
Were you talking on the phone? No, I wasn't.
Carly was crying when I saw her.
Was it raining at three o'clock yesterday? Yes, it was.
We were sitting in the garden when it happened.
Were they talking about exams?
No, they weren't. They were talking about a film.

- We often use the Past continuous and the Past simple in the same sentence. We use the Past continuous for the background activity or situation and the Past simple for the shorter action, e.g. *We were standing at the bus stop when we heard a loud noise.*
- We form the Past continuous with *was/were* + present participle (*-ing* form) of the verb.

- There are rules for forming the present participle:
  – We usually add *-ing* to the verb, e.g. *read/reading, walk/walking, go/going, play/playing.*
  – With verbs ending in one *e*, we drop the *e* and add *-ing*, e.g. *ride – riding, write – writing.*
- With some verbs ending in a consonant, we double the consonant and add *-ing*, e.g. *run – running, sit – sitting, swim – swimming, get – getting.*

2

We have to check in at 2.15

Vocabulary

1 Use the pictures to complete the crossword.

Across

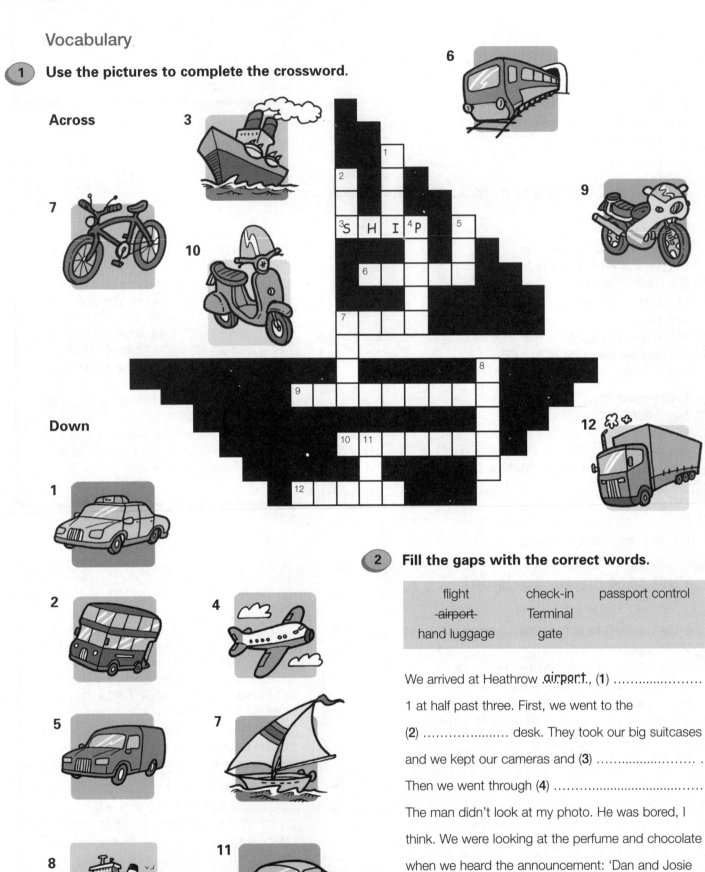

Down

2 Fill the gaps with the correct words.

flight	check-in	passport control
~~airport~~	Terminal	
hand luggage	gate	

We arrived at Heathrow .airport., (**1**) …………………
1 at half past three. First, we went to the
(**2**) ……………….. desk. They took our big suitcases
and we kept our cameras and (**3**) ……………………. .
Then we went through (**4**) ………………………………
The man didn't look at my photo. He was bored, I
think. We were looking at the perfume and chocolate
when we heard the announcement: 'Dan and Josie
Gray, passengers on (**5**) …………… AZ 21 to Rome,
please go immediately to (**6**) …………… number 33.'

16

Dialogue work

3 **Complete the dialogue with the sentences.**

Rachel Come on, Becky. Let's go and buy some presents.

Becky I have to find my passport first.

Rachel Where did you put it?

Becky (1) ....
....

Rachel Did you give it to Mike?

Becky (2) ....
....

Rachel Don't panic. We'll find it. We won't leave you in Italy!

Becky (3) ....

Rachel I've got an idea. Look in your suitcase. I bet it's there.

Becky (4) ....
....

Rachel You probably packed it with your clothes. Now let's go.

Becky (5) ....
....

Rachel Now what's the problem?

Becky (6) ....

- Amazing! How did it get in there?
- Aaarh! Where, oh where is it?
- Did I give you my purse?
- I have to find my passport first.
- No, I didn't. I had it in my hand a minute ago.
- That's the problem. I don't know.
- Err…can you wait a minute?

Grammar practice

4 **Write pairs of sentences with *must* and *mustn't*.**

Be here by eleven. Don't be late.

You must be here by eleven. You mustn't be late.

1 Go to bed early. Don't be tired for the exam.

....

....

2 Be quiet. Don't make a noise.

....

....

3 Wear white shorts for the tournament. Don't wear a tracksuit.

....

....

....

4 Turn your mobile phone off. Don't use it in the hospital.

....

....

....

5 Read the questions first. Don't write anything yet.

....

....

....

5 **Complete the sentences about their jobs. Use *has to / have to* or *doesn't have to / don't have to*.**

pop singer

She ..has to.. have a good voice.

She ..doesn't have to.. speak a lot of languages.

She often ....has to....... work at night.

football players

They .... practise a lot.

They .... be good at Maths.

They .... travel.

They .... use a computer.

taxi driver

She .... wear a uniform.

She .... work at night.

She .... know the town.

She .... enjoy driving.

school teacher

He .... like children.

He .... work at night.

He .... travel.

He .... stand a lot.

6 Complete the sentences with the correct form of *have to* and a verb.

be	cycle	~~get up~~	have
learn	take		wear

My father ..*has to get up*.. at six thirty on weekdays to be at work by eight.

1 I'm tired, Mum. .... I ....…….. the dog for a walk?

2 .... your sister ...…….......................…… a uniform at her school?

3 You ...……..........…...........……. a passport to go from England to Scotland. They are both in Britain.

4 My friend Justin ……........................…............ to school now. He's got a new scooter, lucky thing.

5 Sandra's parents are really strict. She ....…........ home by nine o'clock on Saturday evening.

7 Complete the sentences with *mustn't* or *doesn't have to / don't have to.*

You ...*mustn't*.... go swimming after a big meal. It's dangerous.

It's Sunday tomorrow so she ..*doesn't have to*.. get up early. She can stay in bed until eleven.

1 He ……..........................….............. pay. I've got a free ticket for him.

2 They …...…........... make a noise. Ben is sleeping.

3 We ……........................…....... join after-school clubs but we all like being in them.

4 There's lots of time. We ……..........................…. run to the bus stop.

5 You …......…............ tell Maria. It's our secret, OK?

6 His train is at ten. He …............................ be late.

7 She can bring a friend to the party but she ....

8 Take those dirty football boots off. You …….........…....... wear them in the house.

8 What do you have to do at home? Write three sentences about things you have to do and three sentences about things you don't have to do.

I have to take the dog for walks. ....
I don't have to cook dinner. ....

1 ....
....

2 ....
....

3 ....
....

4 ....
....

5 ....
....

6 ....
....

9 Complete the e-mail with the correct form of the Past simple of the verb *be.*

Hi Luke,

Where ...*were*.... you at six o'clock? I phoned but you (**1**)…............. in. How (**2**)…............ your holiday? Mine (**3**)…............. great. The food (**4**)…............. excellent. The beaches (**5**)…............ great and the girls (**6**)…............. beautiful. The first day there (**7**)…......…........ any sun but after that the weather (**8**)…............. perfect. We (**9**)…............. in a hotel by the sea. The view from my window (**10**)…............. amazing. There (**11**)…............. only one problem. There (**12**)…......…........ any tennis courts. (**13**)…............. your exam results OK? Mine (**14**)…......................... too bad. My parents (**15**)…............. quite pleased with me for a change!

Ciao for now, Dan

10 **Complete the e-mail with the Past simple of the verbs.**

Hi Dan,

I .got.. (get) back from Cornwall this morning and (1)....................... (find) your e-mail. Good news about the exams, mate. I (2)........................ (do) OK too. I (3)........................ (have) a brilliant holiday camping in Newquay. I (4)........................ (go) with Sam and Paul. In the end Jack (5).............................. (not come) with us. We (6)....................... (stay) at a campsite on the beach. We (7)........................ (meet) some girls from Fulham and (8)........................ (spend) a lot of time with them. The weather (9)........................ (not be) very good but at least it (10)............................. (not rain). Sam and I (11)........................ (cook) in the evenings. I (12)................. (make) spaghetti once but it (13)........................ (take) hours! Next time I'm buying it in tins. Paul (14)........................ (not want) to cook so he (15)... (have to) do the washing up every night! We (16).................................... (not sleep) very much at night. We (17).................... (sit) around on the beach and (18)................................. (talk) for hours. (19)............................. (you meet) any nice girls in Spain? What (20).......................... (you do) there in the evenings? (21)............................. (you / go) surfing there? When (22)................................. (you get) back?

Hope to C U soon.

Luke

11 **Complete the sentences in the Past continuous.**

You **were laughing**..... (laugh) in your sleep last night.

1 What .... (you do) yesterday at three o'clock?

2 .... (she wear) her new earrings at Jade's party?

3 We .... (not talk) about you.

4 We .... (talk) about Tracy's cousin.

5 It .... (not rain) at ten this morning.

6 Why .... (Liam write) in his diary at six this morning?

7 He .... (not write) in it. He .... (draw) a picture of his surfboard!

12 **Put the verbs in the Past simple or the Past continuous.**

Last year I ..**was staying**.. (stay) with my friend Megan in York. Her house is very old. One night I (1)............................. (read) in bed. Suddenly I (2)......................... (hear) a boy's voice. The boy (3)............................. (sing) an old song called *Greensleeves*. I (4)...................... (get) out of bed and (5)............................. (open) the door of my room. There was nobody there. In the morning I (6)........................ (ask) Megan, '(7)................ ....(you / sing) in the middle of the night?' 'No,' she said. 'Why? (8)............................. (you / hear) a boy singing *Greensleeves*?' 'Yes,' I (9).................... (answer). 'Who is he?' 'That's our ghost,' she said. 'He's called Tom. He (10)..................... (die) in your bedroom a hundred years ago.'

2 Culture spot

Charles Dickens

In the 19th century British people loved novels. There were lots of book shops and libraries and people had plenty of time to read. Some novelists wrote their books in episodes. People bought one episode a month. It was cheaper than a whole book.

Charles Dickens (1812–1870) wrote novels in this way. He ended each episode with something very exciting so people wanted to buy the next episode. He became the most popular novelist of his time. His books were exciting and funny but they also had a lot of serious messages. He often wrote about poor people and their difficult lives. When people read Dickens's books, they began to understand the problems of the poor.

Charles Dickens knew about the lives of poor people because his own family was poor. His father was in prison for six months because he didn't have enough money to pay his bills. Charles went to work in a shoe polish factory when he was only 12.

Oliver Twist is one of Dickens's most famous novels. Oliver Twist lives in an orphanage because he hasn't got any parents. The orphanage is cold and the children are hungry. When Oliver asks for more food, he gets into a lot of trouble. He leaves the orphanage and goes to London. He meets a man called Fagin. Fagin has a group of children who take money and jewellery from people in the street. Then Fagin keeps the money and the jewellery. Oliver doesn't want to work for him but he has to. Oliver has a lot of adventures but the story has a happy ending.

Dickens also wrote *A Christmas Carol*. It's the story of a very mean man called Scrooge. He pays his workers really badly. Even at Christmas he doesn't give them extra money. One of his workers is called Bob Cratchit. His son, Tiny Tim, is ill and can't walk. The Cratchit family has a very hard life. Then, on Christmas Eve, three ghosts visit Scrooge. He is very scared and he changes. He starts to be kind and generous and he gives presents to everyone. Today we still call a mean person 'a scrooge'.

1 ...　　　　2 ...　　　　3 ...

1 **Read the text about Charles Dickens, then match the captions and the pictures.**

a) Scrooge sees one of the ghosts.

b) Charles Dickens wrote very popular novels.

c) Oliver asks for more food in the orphanage.

Vocabulary

2 **Find the words for:**

a period of 100 years ...century................................

a type of book ....

a person who writes this type of book ....

a part of a story ....

the opposite of funny ....

the opposite of rich ....

something for cleaning shoes ....

a place for children who have no family ....

the opposite of generous ....

the night before Christmas ....

3 **Write short answers to the questions.**

When was Dickens born?

1812..

1 When did he die?

....

2 Why didn't people buy complete books in those days?

....

3 Why did Dickens's father have problems?

....

4 How old was Dickens when he got his first job?

....

5 Why does Oliver get into trouble at the orphanage?

....

6 Who does Bob Cratchit work for?

....

7 Who is Tiny Tim?

....

8 What does Scrooge see on Christmas Eve?

....

Portfolio

4 **Write about you and reading.**

1 Do you prefer reading books or magazines?

....

2 What's your favourite book of all time?

....

3 What's your favourite magazine?

....

4 Do you buy books or borrow them?

....

5 What kind of books do you like best? (*Novels? Books about science/sport/famous people/ history?*)

....

6 How do you usually choose your books? (*Look at the pictures? Copy friends? Read a few pages?*)

....

7 When do you usually read? (*In bed? At weekends?*)

....

8 What was the last book you read?

....

9 What was it like?

....

....

Let's read

Welcome to the Book Club

1 **What did they think of *Oliver Twist*? Read the conversation and write the correct letter in each box.**

Presenter: Welcome to the Book Club. We're here to talk about *Oliver Twist* which you all read last week. What did you all think of it? Sara?

Sara: Before I read it I didn't know anything about London in the nineteenth century. Now I know quite a lot. I learned a lot from it.

Presenter: Lucy?

Lucy: I enjoyed it, It made me laugh a lot.

Presenter: Dan?

Dan: It was OK but I didn't finish it, I'm afraid. I read half of it. I prefer shorter books.

Presenter: Ben?

Ben: I didn't understand the English. There were a lot of strange words.

Presenter: Amy?

Amy: I loved it. I couldn't put it down. I started it on Friday evening and finished it on Sunday evening.

Sara	d	**a)**	It was difficult.
Lucy		**b)**	It was exciting.
Dan		**c)**	It was funny.
Ben		**d)**	It was interesting.
Amy		**e)**	It was terrible.
		f)	It was too long.
		g)	It was frightening.

Let's check

Vocabulary check

1 **Match the transport words to the sentences.**

| bike | cab | coach | motorbike | ~~ship~~ |
| boat | car | lorry | plane | train |

It travels across the sea. .ship.........................

1 It goes on roads. You have to have a ticket to travel on it. ....

2 You get on it at an airport. ....

3 Children can ride it. ....

4 It carries heavy boxes and other things on roads. ....

5 It's smaller than a ship. ....

6 It's another word for a taxi. ....

7 Only one or two people can go on it. ....

8 You get on it at a railway station. ....

9 Most families have got one. ....

Grammar check

2 **Circle the correct words for each sentence.**

We ... his passport in the car yesterday.

A find   **B found**   **C** finding

1 She doesn't ... go by coach. She can take the train.

A have to   **B** need   **C** must

2 They must ... make a noise.

A not   **B** have   **C** to

3 I ... score a goal.

A wasn't   **B** haven't   **C** didn't

4 You ... me perfume last summer.

A buy   **B** buying   **C** bought

5 What ... for breakfast yesterday?

A had you   **B** you had   **C** did you have

6 They ... upset about the match.

A were   **B** was   **C** did

7 Who were you ... to after the film yesterday?

A talked   **B** talking   **C** talk

8 'I wrote to Emma today.' 'So ... Joey.'

A do   **B** was   **C** did

9 I have ... the dog for a walk now.

A to take   **B** taking   **C** take

3 **Correct the mistake in each sentence.**
/\ = there's a word missing; X = change one word; ↳ = change the order of two words; * = you must delete one word.

I have buy a present for my sister. /\
I have to buy a present for my sister.

1 You two does not have to go yet. **X**
....

2 What have we got do for homework? /\
....
....

3 Who you were waiting for outside the cinema? ↳
....
....

4 Who was drew this picture in my notebook? *
....
....

5 I didn't found any nice chocolates in that shop. **X**
....
....

4 **Make sentences by putting the words in order.**

airport / arrived / and / at / check-in desk / to / the / the / We / went
We arrived at the airport and went to the check-in desk.

1 Do / have / I / in / match / on / play / Saturday / the / to / ?
....
....

2 bed / did / dirty / football / leave / my / on / shirt / you / your / Why / ?
....
....
....

3 a call / got / I / I / mobile / my / on / phone / the / match / while / was / watching
....
....
....

Extra!

1 **Read the text and answer the questions.**

The Brontës

Jane Eyre and *Wuthering Heights* are two of the most popular novels in English literature. *Jane Eyre* is by Charlotte Brontë and *Wuthering Heights* is the work of her sister, Emily.

The six Brontë children grew up in the small village of Haworth in Yorkshire. Their father, Patrick, was a church of England priest in Haworth. Their mother, Maria, died in 1821, when the oldest child was only seven.

A few years after their mother's death, the four oldest girls went to a church boarding school. It was a terrible experience and ended in disaster. The school was cold, the food was bad and the teachers were very strict. Eleven-year-old Maria and ten-year-old Elizabeth Brontë became very ill. Their father brought the four girls home but Maria and Elizabeth never got better. They died of tuberculosis a few months later.

From 1824 to 1831, the four surviving Brontë children, Charlotte, Branwell (the only boy), Emily and Anne stayed at home and had lessons with their father and their aunt. They didn't have friends outside their home and they didn't meet the children in the village. It was a very quiet life but the children were close to each other in age and they loved using their imagination. They enjoyed reading and wrote little books in tiny writing for Branwell's toy soldiers to read.

Later on, the three girls worked as teachers. Charlotte and Anne were private teachers to the children of rich families.

The dining room in Haworth

Then, for a short time, Charlotte and Emily taught at a girls' school in Brussels. None of them enjoyed teaching and, when their aunt died and left them some money, they decided to stay at their family home, writing.

Charlotte's *Jane Eyre,* Emily's *Wuthering Heights* and Anne's *Agnes Grey* were published in 1847. But the Brontë family didn't have long to celebrate. In 1848, Branwell died of tuberculosis. Nine months later, Emily and Anne were dead of the same illness.

Jane Eyre was a great success. Charlotte Brontë made quite a lot of money from it and became quite famous. She wrote several more novels before marrying in 1854. Tragically, she died a year later at the age of 39.

The Brontës' house in Haworth is now a museum. You can see the dining room where the three young women spent their evenings discussing the characters and plots of their novels and doing their writing. And you can get an idea of the everyday life of this very unusual family.

1 Who wrote *Wuthering Heights*?

2 How many children were there in the Brontë family?

3 Where did they live?

4 What was the church boarding school like?

5 At what age did Maria and Elizabeth Brontë die?

6 How many brothers did the Brontë sisters have?

7 Who taught the Brontë children after Maria and Elizabeth's deaths?

8 How did the Brontë sisters get enough money to stop working as teachers?

9 What is the Brontës' house now?

10 In which room did the Brontës write their novels?

11 What is your favourite book? Write two sentences saying what it's about.

12 Do you prefer books or films? Why?

Answers

1 ....
....
2 ....
3 ....
....
4 ....
....
5 ....
....
6 ....
7 ....
....
8 ....
....
9 ....
10 ....
11 ....
....
....
12 ....
....
....
....

Tip

- Don't write the shortest possible answers. Try to show off your English! For example, in the dialogue on the right, one of the questions is *Where did you go for your last holidays?* **The shortest possible answer would be the name of the place, e.g.** *Paris*. **But you can make your answer more interesting, e.g.** *I went to Paris with my brother. We stayed with some French friends.* **But don't write too much either.**

2 **Complete your part of the dialogue.**

Interviewer	I'm writing an article for a teenage magazine. Can I ask you a few questions?
You	Yes, of course. ....
Interviewer	What sort of things do you have to do to help at home?
You	....
Interviewer	Really? So you have to do quite a lot. And how long does it take you to do the washing up every evening?
You	....
Interviewer	Are there any jobs you hate doing?
You	....
Interviewer	I don't like cleaning the bathroom either! How often do you have to clean it?
You	....
Interviewer	How much pocket money do you get?
You	....
Interviewer	That's a lot! What do you spend it on?
You	....
Interviewer	And after all that, do you manage to save any of it?
You	....
Interviewer	What are you saving up for?
You	....
Interviewer	So who are you going to go with on this trip?
You	....
Interviewer	Where did you go for your last holidays?
You	....
Interviewer	What did you do there?
You	....
Interviewer	Thanks very much for your time.

GRAMMAR FILE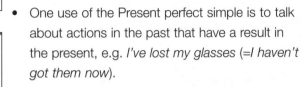

Present perfect simple

Affirmative

Long form	**Short form**
I have started.	I've started.
You have started.	You've started.
She has started.	She's started.
He has started.	He's started.
It has started.	It's started.
We have started.	We've started.
You have started.	You've started.
They have started.	They've started.

Negative

Long form	**Short form**
I have not started.	I haven't started.
You have not started.	You haven't started.
She has not started.	She hasn't started.
He has not started.	He hasn't started.
It has not started.	It hasn't started.
We have not started.	We haven't started.
You have not started.	You haven't started.
They have not started.	They haven't started.

Questions

Have I started?
Have you started?
Has she started?
Has he started?
Has it started?
Have we started?
Have you started?
Have they started?

Short answers

Affirmative	**Negative**
Yes, I have.	No, I haven't.
Yes, you have.	No, you haven't.
Yes, she has.	No, she hasn't.
Yes, he has.	No, he hasn't.
Yes, it has.	No, it hasn't.
Yes, we have.	No, we haven't.
Yes, you have.	No, you haven't.
Yes, they have.	No, they haven't.

Wh? questions

What have I / you / we / they started?
What has she / he / it started?

- One use of the Present perfect simple is to talk about actions in the past that have a result in the present, e.g. *I've lost my glasses* (=*I haven't got them now*).
- We also use it to give news about something that has happened recently, e.g. *She's bought a new scooter.*
- We never use the Present perfect simple with time phrases like *yesterday, last month/year/ last week, on Sunday, in June.* With these time phrases, we use the Past simple.
- We form the Present perfect simple with the verb *have* and the past participle.
- In the third person singular, the short form of *has* is *'s*, e.g. *She's finished her project. Is it raining? No, it's stopped.*

- The past participle of all regular verbs is the same as the Past simple:

Past simple	Past participle
played	*played*
started	*started*
lived	*lived*
cry	*cried*

Irregular past participle

Infinitive	Past simple	Past participle
be	was	been
become	became	become
come	came	come
do	did	done
eat	ate	eaten
fall	fell	fallen
go	went	gone/been
see	saw	seen
swim	swam	swum
write	wrote	written

- The past participle of some irregular verbs is the same as the Past simple.

Infinitive	Past simple	Past participle
lose	*lost*	*lost*
have	*had*	*had*
make	*made*	*made*
meet	*met*	*met*
win	*won*	*won*

- With some irregular verbs, the past participle is different from the Past simple. There is a list of irregular verbs on page 135 of the Student's Book.

Present perfect simple with *ever* and *never*

Have you ever seen a ghost? No, I've never seen a ghost.

Has your brother ever talked in his sleep? Yes, he has.

I've never won a competition.

She's never eaten in a Chinese restaurant.

- We use *ever* and *never* with the Present perfect simple. We use *ever* in questions, e.g. *Have you ever fallen off a horse?* We can use *never* to answer them, e.g. *No, I've never been on a horse so I've never fallen off one.*

been and *gone*

They look well. Have they **been** on holiday?

'You look tired.' 'I am tired. I've **been** at the gym.'

There's a new cinema in our street. Have you **been** to it?

They aren't here. They've **gone** on holiday.

Dave has **gone** to the gym. He'll be back in an hour and a half.

My mother isn't here. She's **gone** to the cinema.

- The verb *go* has two past participles: *been* and *gone*.
- We use *gone* to say that someone has gone away and hasn't yet returned, e.g. *Zoe is on holiday. She has gone to Thailand.* (= She is in Thailand now.)
- We use *been* to say that someone has been away and has now returned, e.g. *I saw Liam in the park. He has been to Thailand.* (= He went to Thailand but now he is back.)

3

We've had an e-mail from Tommaso

Vocabulary

1 Use the pictures to complete the crossword.

Across

1   3   4   6   7

Down

1   2   5

2 Complete the entries in the chart for yourself.

My post code ....

My e-mail address ....

My mobile phone number ....

Emergency services ....

Directory enquiries ....

International code for my country ....

International code for Britain ....

International code for ....

Dialogue work

3 Complete the dialogue with these words.

| card | Europe | letter | post office |
| envelope | kisses | photo | ~~stamps~~ |

Adam   Have you got any ...stamps...?

Becky   I've got one. Who have you written to?

Adam   Do I have to tell you?

Becky   Yes, if you want this stamp.

Adam   Well I've made a (**1**)...................... for my gran. It's her birthday tomorrow.

Becky   OK. Here you are.

Adam   Thanks. Now I need a stamp for (**2**)................ for my letter to Tommaso. I suppose I'll have to go to the (**3**)....................................

Becky   Have you closed the (**4**)...........................?

Adam   No.

Becky   Can you put this (**5**).................... of me and Rachel in with your (**6**)....................?

Adam   OK.

Becky   Who's the third letter to?

Adam   Eloisa.

Becky   That's funny. You haven't put any (**7**)................... on the envelope.

Grammar practice

4 **Put the verbs in the Present perfect. They are all regular.**

I ...<u>have tried</u>...... (try) all the pizzas on this menu. Pizza Surprise is the best.

1 Elly .... (save) a lot of money. She's going to buy a camera.

2 My aunt .... (move) house. She lives in Brighton now.

3 They .... (decide) to go and live in Spain.

4 She's really annoyed because somebody ....(open) her letter from Dan.

5 We .... (listen) to all the songs on this CD. The one called Kisses is the best.

6 She................................. (look) everywhere but she still can't find her passport.

7 Justin .... (invite) thirty people to his barbecue. It will be fun.

8 I .... (start) this book three times but I always get bored at page 20!

5 **Write the correct verb in each gap in the Present perfect. They are all irregular.**

do	go	lose	see
buy	~~make~~	meet	eat

We.<u>'ve made</u>...... some pancakes. Would you like one?

1 I........................ all my homework. I'm going out now.

2 She............................... that film twice. She doesn't want to see it again.

3 We can't make sandwiches. Fred .... all the bread and cheese.

4 You............................ my uncle. He's called Scott.

5 Luke.................................... the keys. How are we going to get into the house?

6 Her parents .... to Australia. They're coming back in February.

7 My dad .... me a new tennis racket. It's great!

6 **Choose the correct prompts and complete the responses in the Present perfect.**

Does Sylvie like her new school?

I don't know because <u>she hasn't written to me</u>.

1 Are Tim and Andy having fun in Spain?

Probably but ....
....

2 We got a postcard from Rosie.

Lucky you! ....

3 Does your mum like the books?

She says so but ....
....

4 What was the cake like?

We don't know ....

5 What do you think of Dan's cousins?

I don't know. ....

6 What's wrong with the cat?

She's hungry. ....
....

7 Would you like a sandwich?

Yes, please. ....
....

8 What's his new camera like?

I don't know. ....
....

- I (not / meet) them.
- I (not / see) any of his photos.
- She (not / have) her breakfast.
- I (not / eat) anything today.
- she (not / read) them all.
- ~~she (not / write) to me.~~
- She (not / send) us one.
- we (not / hear) from them.
- We (not / try) it.

3

7 Match the statements to the questions. Write the questions in the Present perfect.

It's Selina's birthday tomorrow.

[b.] .....What have you bought her?.....................

1 They've bought the pumpkins.

[…] ....

2 Thank you for the delicious meal.

[…] ....

3 I'm going out with Lily now, Mum.

[…] ....

4 Can you lend me your glasses for a minute?

[…] ....

5 We can probably have the party at Jamie's house.

[…] ....

6 Ben's back at school now.

[…] ....

7 Carly doesn't live in England now.

[…] ....

8 I gave you the keys.

[…] ....

a) (he be) ill?
b) ~~What (you buy) her?~~
c) (you done) your homework?
d) (you have) enough to eat?
e) (you lose) yours again?
f) Really? What (I do) with them?
g) (he ask) his parents?
h) (they make) the lanterns?
i) Where (she move) to?

There are two Present perfect forms for the verb *go*:

have/has gone and *have/has been.*

We use *have/has gone* when the person has gone somewhere and has not returned.

'Where's Georgie?' 'She's gone to the park.'

8 Complete the sentences with the Present perfect, using *been* or *gone.*

'Is Alex in?' 'No, he isn't. He...'s.gone... to a football match.'

'You're late home. Where have you been?' 'We.'ve.been.. to a party.'

1 They.....................….…….. to France. They be back in a week.

2 'What's China like?' 'I don't know. I …....................….….n't….......................…. there.

3 Sandro …….….....................…. to the beach. He be back around six.

4 'I want to go to Edinburgh.' 'I …......................… there twice. It's a beautiful city.'

5 You …….....................…….… to a lot of parties th week. Why don't you stay at home tonight?

6 The Redferns aren't here. They …......................… on holiday.

7 Let's go sightseeing. ………….. you …………… to The Tower of London?

8 'Is Liza here or ………… she………… to football practice?'

9 Look, the Mertons are in their garden. They …………..n't ……….................. to Liverpool for the weekend.

10 You look great. ………… you…………… on holiday?

We use *have/has been* when the person has made a visit and has now returned.

'Where have you been?' 'We've been to the cinema.'

9 Write questions with *Have you ever ...?* Then answer the questions.

ARE YOU CRAZY ABOUT PARTIES?

(invite) more than 40 people to a party

1 (dance) on a table at a party?

2 (go) to a party in your pyjamas?

3 (be) the last person to leave a party?

4 (have) three invitations in one week?

5 (make) a lot of noise at a party?

6 (stay) up all night at a party?

7 (fall) off a chair at a party?

8 (play) in a band at a party?

9 (lose) your shoes at a party?

10 (clean) the house after a party?

Have you ever invited more than 40 people to a party? No

1 ....

2 ....

3 ....

4 ....

5 ....

6 ....

7 ....

8 ....

9 ....

10 ....

10 Use the prompts to write sentences in the Present perfect.

Josh (try) snowboarding (✓) surfing (✗)

Josh has tried snowboarding but he hasn't tried surfing.

1 Lila (have) a party in her garden (✓) one on the beach (✗) ....

2 I (be) a plane (✓) a ship (✗)

3 You (write) a story (✓) a song (✗)

4 I (work) in a café (✓) a shop (✗)

5 They (buy) a dog (✓) a horse (✗)

6 My grandmother (win) a bike (✓) a TV (✗)

7 I (go) to Denmark (✓) Sweden (✗)

8 She (see) Andrea (✓) Sylvie (✗)

A

Dear Alexander

I hope you aren't going to be cold in the tent. Are you going to have breakfast with us in the dining room tomorrow morning? Please don't cook in the tent. It's very dangerous. When do you think you are going to come back to your bedroom?

Lots of love

Mother

B

Dear Mum

Don't worry! I've got my **sleeping bag** and my **duvet**. And I'm certainly not going to cook breakfast (or myself) in the tent. I've got cereal and milk here for breakfast and a **thermos** of hot tea. I've also helped myself to a carton of orange juice from the fridge. I hope you don't mind. I've got my **alarm clock** and I'll wake myself up for school. I find it very peaceful in my tent and of course I can listen to music all night and read if I want. I've got an excellent **torch** and plenty of **batteries**. I've got my CD player out here and I've used Dad's **extension lead** to get electricity. So you see I've been very organised.

The great thing is - nobody tells me to tidy the tent.

Your loving son,

Alex

C

Can I move into your tent with you? I am really sick of living with my family. Can we talk about it after this Maths lesson?

Luke

Sorry, mate. My tent is for (one) person only.

Alex

D

Garden Campsite

A 14-year-old boy has moved out of his bedroom and is living in a tent in the garden of his family home. His mother, Mrs Wilson says, 'We have not had any fights or arguments at home. We all get on very well in our family. Alexander has always loved outdoor life and he enjoys living in the garden. But I am sure he will come back to the house soon.'

E

Hi Alex

I'm glad you are still enjoying life in your tent. Are you going to stay there forever? Can I have your old bedroom? It's bigger and lighter than mine. And Mum has made new **curtains** for the windows and Dad has made a new shelf for your CDs. I don't understand them. Why are they doing things to your room when you live in a tent now? Anyway, is it OK for me to take your bedroom?

Your sister,

Rosie

F

Dear Rosie

I am afraid you can't have my old bedroom. I'll phone you tomorrow and explain.

Alex

Read

1 **Read the texts to find answers to these questions.**

1 Where is Alex living at the moment?

....

2 What has he got to keep him warm at night?

....

3 Who wants to join him?

....

4 How old is Alex?

....

5 What does Rosie want to do?

....

6 What's Alex's answer to her?

....

7 What do you think Alex is going to say to Rosie on the plane?

....

....

....

2 **Guess the meaning of these words from their context. Write the correct word under each picture.**

sleeping bag	alarm clock	extension lead
duvet	torch	~~curtains~~
thermos	batteries	

1 curtains ....

2 ....
....

3 ....
....

4 ....
....

5 ....

6 ....

7 ....

8 ....

Write

3 **Write an e-mail from Alex to a friend about his time in the tent. Use these ideas:**

Hi ....

Last month I moved out of my bedroom into a tent in the garden. I decided to move because ....

....

....

Life in the tent was fun at first.
I ....

....

....

But after three weeks I was bored with the tent because ....

....

....

So I moved back to my bedroom. I really like being at home now because ....

....

....

Write to me soon, Alex

Study tips

4 **We learn better when we understand why we are doing something. Look at the exercises in this unit and find an exercise where you:**

	Page	Exercise
practise new vocabulary		
practise useful phrases		
learn some new words		
practise using grammar		
look for answers in a text		

3 Talk time

1 Complete the dialogue with these phrases.

- Don't panic • I hope • ~~It says~~
- See you • straight after

Mel   What time do we have to get the coach?

Chloe   Hmm. Let me look at the information sheet. ..It says.. the coach leaves from school at ten fifteen.

Mel   But my guitar lesson only finishes at ten.

Chloe   Is your lesson at home?

Mel   Yes.

Chloe   Well you can cycle to school (**1**)............................... your guitar lesson.

Mel   (**2**)............................... Miss Miller isn't going to be late.

Chloe   Who's Miss Miller?

Mel   She's my guitar teacher. And I don't think she's got a watch! She's always late. I really don't want to miss the coach because of her.

Chloe   (**3**)............................... . Everything's going to be OK.

Mel   You hope!

Chloe   (**4**)............................... at the school gates at ten fifteen.

Mel   Bye!

2 Match the questions to the answers.

[.c.] Why is Ben so happy today?
1 [...] At last! Why are you so late?
2 [...] What's she done wrong?
3 [...] Where did you see Craig?
4 [...] Cristina? Who is Cristina?
5 [...] Why do you look so hot?

a) He was on his way to the football pitch.
b) You know, she's the girl from Mexico.
c) ~~He's won a trip to New York.~~
d) Sorry, we got on the wrong bus.
e) She's left her Maths homework at home again.
f) I've run all the way from Joey's house.

Let's check

Vocabulary check

1 **Match the words to the clues.**

address	mobile phone	post code
ambulance	net	post office
envelope	post box	~~stamps~~
international code	postcards	website

Some people collect them. .stamps..................

1 An e-mail .... always has @ in it.

2 Can I borrow your ...., please? I need to call my mother.

3 Help! There's been an accident. Call an ....

4 I was surfing the .... yesterday and I found a great .... with information about pop stars.

5 In Britain a .... always has ....letters and numbers. Mine is W6 9DH.

6 You can't put that letter in the .... It hasn't got a stamp on it yet.

7 People on holiday often send these. ....

8 The .... for Italy is 00 39 and for Britain it's 00 44.

9 When you've written a letter you put it in an ....

10 You can post letters and buy stamps here. ....

Grammar check

2 **Correct the mistake in each sentence.**
/\ = there's a word missing; X = change one word; ⤷ = change the order of two words; * = you must delete one word.

Have ever they tried windsurfing? ⤷
Have they ever tried windsurfing?
....

1 Why she has written her name in my book? ⤷
....
....

2 What you done with my stamps? /\
....

3 Nice to see you – where have you been gone ? *
....
....

4 We haven't never met your Australian cousins. X
....
....

5 You've gone to Ireland – what's it like? X
....
....

3 **Circle the correct words for each sentence.**

Who has ... all the orange juice?
A drank   **B** drinking   **C** drunk

1 ... she bought a new tennis racket?
A Was   **B** Did   **C** Has

2 The room looks great. Who ... the table?
A was clearing   **B** has cleared   **C** did clear

3 We've ... to Kirsty about the tournament.
A wrote   **B** write   **C** written

4 Has she ever ... a race?
A lose   **B** lost   **C** losing

5 We have ... all the Harry Potter films.
A saw   **B** see   **C** seen

6 They've ... been to Venice.
A ever   **B** to   **C** never

7 I'm bored. I ... done anything all day.
A haven't   **B** didn't   **C** have

8 Elly and Rob are out. They've ... to the cinema.
A gone   **B** been   **C** went

9 Fantastic! I have ... a trip to France.
A win   **B** winning   **C** won

10 Why has she ... to bed? Is she OK?
A been   **B** gone   **C** went

GRAMMAR FILE

Present perfect simple with *just, already, yet*

just

We've just seen Sabina.

I've just bought these sunglasses. What do you think of them?

Adam has just gone out. He'll be back in an hour.

You look white. Have you just seen a ghost?

already

I've already had my lunch.

Nina has already seen the play.

yet

Have you had lunch yet?

Has Mel finished her English project yet?

I haven't asked Dave about the picnic yet.

Sara hasn't paid me for the ticket yet.

- We use *just* + the Present perfect when we talk about something that happened a short time ago, e.g. *I'm not hungry. I've just had lunch.* (= a short time ago)

- The position of *just* is after the auxiliary *have* and before the past participle, e.g. *Dan has just gone out. I've just seen a huge dog in our garden.*

- We use *already* + the Present perfect when we talk about something that happened before we expected it, e.g. *It's only seven o'clock but Sandy has already gone to bed.* (= before I expected). *'Karen, this is Ellie.' 'I know. We've already met.'*

- The position of *already* is after the auxiliary *have* and before the past participle, e.g. *Melissa has already finished her History project, lucky thing.*

- We use *yet* + the Present perfect when we talk or ask about something that has not happened so far, e.g. *I haven't told my parents about the accident yet. Have you bought a present for Leila yet?*

- We can use *yet* in questions and negative sentences. We can't use *yet* in affirmative sentences.

- The position of *yet* is at the end of the sentence, e.g. *I haven't used my new tennis racket yet.* NOT: *I haven't used yet my new tennis racket.*

Present perfect with *for* or *since*

for

I've been here for an hour.

Daniel's lived in Liverpool for five months.

We've had our dog for three weeks.

I've known you for three months.

I haven't seen him for ages.

She hasn't phoned for days.

since

I've been here since one o'clock.

Daniel's lived in Liverpool since May.

We've had our dog since 3rd September.

I've known you since July.

I haven't seen him since 2003.

She hasn't phoned since last Monday.

- We use the Present perfect + *for* or *since* to say how long something has lasted, e.g. *I have known him for three years. She has been ill since Friday.*

- We use *for* + a period of time, e.g. *for three days, for two weeks, for one month, for a year, for two minutes, for an hour, for a long time, for ages.*

- We use *since* + the beginning of a period of time, e.g. *since Monday, since January, since the third of March, since 1999, since 9 o'clock, since my birthday, since we arrived.*

Present perfect with *how long, how many times*

How long have you been here?
How long has she known Mike?
How many times have you been to Canada?
How many times has she fallen off her scooter?

- We use *How long* + Present perfect to ask questions about a situation that began in the past but still continues in the present, e.g. *How long have you had that scooter? For three months. How long has she known Martin? Since March.*

- We can also use *How many times* + Present perfect, e.g. *How many times have you been in a helicopter? Three times. How many times has she had a detention this term? Just once.*

Past simple or Present perfect simple?

Past simple
We **saw** her yesterday.
I **did** it last week.
She **arrived** at 2 o'clock.
They **bought** it in 2001.
You **told** me a month ago.
I **didn't go** to school yesterday.
Where **did you go** last summer?
What time **did you get up** this morning?
When **did you see** her?
Shakespeare **wrote** lots of plays.
Princess Diana **died** in a car crash.

Present perfect simple
Look! **I've found** my keys.
Hooray! **I've finished** my homework.
I can't find my glasses. **Have you seen** them?
Amy **has gone** to the shops. She'll be back soon.
I'm tired. **I've been** at work all day.
Have you ever been to Japan?
She's never played table tennis.
Have you heard the new *Darkness* CD yet?
I've already seen her holiday photos.
My sister **has just bought** a hamster.
I've known her since September.
We've been friends for years.
How long have they had that dog?
How many times have you been in a helicopter?

- We use the Past simple to talk about actions that happened and ended in the past, e.g. *Shakespeare wrote lots of plays.*

- We use the Past simple with time phrases like *yesterday, last week/year/month, on Friday, two months/weeks/days ago* and in questions with *When?*, e.g. *When did you see her? I saw her last night. When did you arrive? I arrived ten minutes ago.* We do NOT use the Present perfect with these time expressions.

- We use the Present perfect to talk about actions that started in the past but have an effect now, e.g. *I've lost my keys* (= I can't find them now). *The cat has eaten our dinner* (= we have nothing to eat now).

- We also use the Present perfect to give news about something that has happened recently, e.g. *A Scottish Student has won £1 million.*

- We use the Present perfect with *never, ever, just, already, yet, so far, since, for.* We use the Present perfect with *How long* questions when we expect an answer with *for* or *since*. We use the Present perfect with *How many* questions when the meaning *so far* is understood, e.g. *How many letters have you written today? How many times have you ridden a camel?* (= so far in your life).

Your wish has just come true!

Vocabulary

1 Match the words in the box to the posters.

ballet	This Christmas at the Brighton Playhouse **Snow White** John Davis plays Snow White!!
comedy	
concert	
musical	
opera	
~~pantomime~~	
play	

The Old Vic Theatre

Shakespeare's

Romeo and Juliet

Luciano Pavarotti

sings in

Giuseppe Verdi's **Rigoletto**

pantomime ....   1 ....   2 ....

The National Dance Company presents **Swan Lake** with choreography by Emilia La Jambe

La Scala Orchestra plays Beethoven's **Ninth Symphony**

Mamma Mia with music by **Abba** at the Dominion Theatre You'll love the singing and the dancing.

The funniest show in town. **Billy Batt** talks about his family and other animals. **You WILL laugh!**

3 ....   4 ....   5 ....   6 ....

2 Complete the crossword. Use the letters after each clue.

Across

2 We all wrote the ... of our pantomime. (TRICPS)
5 They act in plays. (ROCTAS)
7 Did you have a big ... in your school play? (TRAP)
8 My ... was amazing. I wore a big green hat and silver trousers. (MESTUOC)
9 I had a fantastic ... . I was at the front of the theatre. (TASE)
10 You can collect your tickets from the ... at six o'clock. (KETTIC EFFICO)
11 The ... loved the opera. They clapped and shouted. (DANCEUIE)

Down

1 You can read about the actors in the ... (EMMGARROP)
2 The actors in a theatre perform on a ... (GESTA)
3 Ladies and gentlemen, tonight's ... of *Cinderella* will begin in three minutes. (CAPERFERMON)
4 You must learn your ... before the dress rehearsal. (ESNIL)
6 A big group of classical musicians. (ACHESTORR)
7 The ... of the play was very simple but it wasn't boring. (LOPT)
9 In the last ... there was a real horse on the stage. (ENECS)

Dialogue work

3 **Complete the dialogue with the correct sentences.**

Mum You're late. Where have you been?

Becky We had an extra rehearsal.
Then I went back to Adam's.

Mum Has he learnt his lines yet?

Becky Yes, he has. (1)...
....

Mum When are you going to do the programmes?

Becky (2)...
I got up at six this morning and I did them on your computer.

Mum You must be tired and hungry.

Becky I am. (3)...
.... Is dinner ready?

Mum Yes. (4)...
.... Help yourself.

Becky Yummy! (5) ....
....

Mum Yes. I ate at six when I got home.

- And his mum has made him a brilliant costume.
- Have you already eaten?
- I haven't eaten anything since breakfast.
- I've already done them.
- I've made lasagne with spinach and cheese.
- ~~Then I went back to Adam's.~~

Grammar practice

4 **There is a list of irregular past participles on page 135 of the Student's Book. Use the phrases to write captions with *just* and the Present perfect.**

- go to the hairdresser's
- have dinner
- lose the match
- see a ghost
- ~~finish her book~~
- speak to Katie
- win £1,000

She's just finished her book.

1 ....
....

2 ....
....

3 ....
....

4 ....
....

5 ....
....

Would you like something to eat?

6 No thanks, I ....
....

5 Use the prompts to write responses in the Present perfect with *already*.

A: I must empty the bin.

B: It's OK. I / empty / it

I've already emptied it.

1 **A:** We should send an invitation to Linda.

B: Don't worry. Dave / send / her / one

....

2 **A:** I have to do my Science project this weekend.

B: Bad luck! I / do / mine

....

3 **A:** I want to go swimming.

B: We / go

....

4 **A:** What do you want for lunch?

B: Nothing, thanks. We / eat

....

5 **A:** Does Bethan want to come to the pantomime?

B: No, she / see it

....

6 **A:** Let's go out when it stops raining.

B: It / stop

....

6 Use the prompts to write questions with the Present perfect and *yet*, and answers with *going to*.

A: you / write to Serena ?

Have you written to Serena yet?

B: write / tomorrow

I'm going to write to her tomorrow.

1 **A:** Claire / buy a hamster?

....

B: buy one / Saturday

....

2 **A:** you / speak to Gary?

....

B: speak / this evening

....

3 **A:** Laura / make the cake?

....

B: make / tomorrow

....

4 **A:** you / take a picture of us?

....

B: take one / in a minute

....

....

7 Look at the checklist for the school play. Write what people have *already* done and what they haven't done *yet*.

SCHOOL PLAY

Tanya and Kate: *finish Ryan's costume* (✗)

Isobel: *take the photos for the programmes* (✓)

1 Sam: *write the programmes* (✓)

2 Tanya: *find a necklace for Kirsty* (✗)

3 Isobel: *check the lights on the stage* (✗)

4 Mark and Dan: *move the piano* (✓)

5 Tom: *speak to Amy about her lines* (✗)

Tanya and Kate haven't finished Ryan's costume yet.

Isobel has already taken the photos for the programmes.

1 ....

....

2 ....

....

3 ....

....

4 ....

....

5 ....

....

8 Use the prompts to write questions in the Present perfect and answers with *for* or *since*.

You / know Jen

How long have you known Jen?

three years

I've known her for three years.

Your grandmother / have that car?

How long has your grandmother had that car?

1999

She's had it since 1999.

1 Sara / be in the bath?

....

....

half an hour

....

2 they / live in Paris?

....

....

four years

....

3 Alex / work at the sports centre?

....

....

July

....

4 you / wear glasses?

....

I was ten

....

5 Amy / have your CDs?

....

....

two weeks

....

6 they / be in Brighton?

....

....

three days

....

9 Present perfect or Past simple? Tick (✓) the four correct sentences. Cross (✗) the five incorrect sentences and write them correctly.

I've just seen a really scary film. [✓.]

Mum wants to go to the new Chinese restaurant. We never went there. [✗.]

1 Bryony didn't speak to me since the party. [...]

2 Has Carol moved house yet? [...]

3 I gave her a watch last week and she already lost it. [...]

4 I'm tired. I've just been to the gym. [...]

5 I've lost my keys. I can't find them anywhere. [...]

6 Sam has come back from Portugal yesterday. [...]

7 We've been to the beach last weekend. [...]

8 What time have you gone to bed last night? [...]

9 Your hair looks nice. What have you done to it? [...]

We've never been there.

• ....

....

• ....

....

• ....

....

• ....

....

• ....

....

10 Write five sentences about you, your friends or family using the Present perfect and *for* or *since*.

Josie has been at this school for two years.

We have had a dog since 1999.

.... had ....

....

........................known ....

....

.... studied ....

....

Culture spot

School in the USA

Hi Zoe

Thanks for your e-mail. Your school sounds **awesome**. I would really like to go to an English boarding school like yours. My school is totally ordinary. So why do you want to know about it?!! Anyway here goes!

I'm in **8th grade** at Alice Deal Junior High, Washington DC. In the US, kids start in 1st grade at age 6 and finish in 12th grade. For 7th through 9th grade you go to Junior High School.

At some schools the kids have to wear uniform. We don't have a uniform but there is a dress code. That means kids shouldn't go to school in baggy skateboarding **pants**, or really short skirts or clothes with holes in them. And kids can't dye their hair crazy colors!

School starts at 8.45 and finishes at 3.15. A lot of kids stay on until 5.30 to play sports or go to the after-school program. That means you can stay at school to do your **assignments**, or go to the computer lab. Last year my Math **grades** were really bad, so I did Math in the after-school program. Now my Math is OK but I still don't like it. My favourite subject is **Phys-ed**.

We do the same subjects as you but we do Spanish instead of French. That's because there are a lot of people in the US who speak Spanish at home. Some schools in Washington DC are totally bilingual in Spanish and English because there are so many Latino kids. Their parents or grandparents are from Central America originally, mainly from El Salvador.

We have lunch in the **cafeteria** at school. The food is OK. Today we had pizza for lunch. We also have a fifteen-minute **recess** in the morning.

One of the best things at my school is the **field trips**. Last week we went on a biology field trip to Kenilworth Aquatic Gardens. It's a national park with a river and lakes. We spent the morning there and ate lunch in the picnic area. There are hundreds of water birds and we also saw turtles, frogs and water snakes. The plants are kind of tropical. There are pink and white flowers in all the lakes. It is totally cool.

Only one week now until the summer **vacation**. Then I'll be free for over ten weeks. I'm going to sailing camp for three weeks with my friend Doug. I can't wait.

Hope you like these photos. Write back!

Danny

1 **Read the letter and find short answers to these questions.**

1 Which country is Zoe's school in?

....

2 Which country does Danny live in?

....

3 Does he wear school uniform?

....

4 Which subject doesn't he like?

....

5 Which language does he study?

....

6 Name three things to see at Kenilworth Aquatic Gardens.

....

2 Write the correct caption under each photo.

1 ....
....

2 ....
....

3 ....
....

4 ....
....

- This is a basketball game at my school.
- This is me outside my school. I'm in the middle.
- This is the school cafeteria.
- It was hard to get this picture. This frog didn't want to sit still!

Vocabulary

3 Match American English words to the British English words.

holiday	year eight	canteen	homework
~~amazing~~	class visit	break	
marks	PE	trousers	

	American English	British English
	awesome	amazing...............
1	eighth grade	....
2	pants	....
3	assignments	....
4	grades	....
5	Phys-ed	....
6	cafeteria	....
7	recess	....
8	field trip	....
9	vacation	....

Portfolio

4 Write about you and school.

1 What's your school called?
....

2 How long have you been there?
....

3 What kind of school is it?
....

4 Do you wear a uniform?
....

5 Is there a dress code? What can/can't you wear?
....

6 What time does your school day start and finish?
....

7 What class are you in?
....

8 How many pupils are there in your class?
....

9 What kind of exams do you do at your school?
....

10 Do you go to any classes after school? What are they?
....

11 What's the best thing about your school?
....

12 What's the worst thing about your school?
....

Let's read

National Park Day

1 Complete the notice with these words:

bags	day	helpers	nearest
clean	friends	~~litter~~	something
collect	games	morning	

NATIONAL PARK DAY

Do you care about your environment?

Do you hate the ..litter..............

in your local park?

Here's your chance to do

(1) .... about it.

Saturday 26th June
is National Park Day

Go to your (2) .... park at eleven o'clock

in the (3) .... Take (4) ....

or family with you. Together we'll (5) ....

sweet papers, drink cans and plastic (6) ....

It'll be a fun (7) .... out. There'll be

(8) .... and races, a free disco and a

barbecue for all the (9) ....

See you there!

Together we can (10) ....

up London's parks.

Let's check

Vocabulary check

1 **What are they talking about? Match the types of show to what people said.**

play	comedy	ballet	~~pantomime~~	concert	opera

Cinderella was a man! **pantomime**............................

1 They were all fantastic dancers. ....

2 I love Verdi. *Aida* is his best. ....

3 I haven't laughed like that for months! ....

4 I liked the piano solo best. ....

5 It was a difficult plot but I enjoyed it. ....

2 **Choose the correct words for the gaps.**

audience	orchestra	scene
costumes	performances	~~seats~~
lines	plot	stage
main character	programme	

'Which are our ..**seats**..?' 'We're B6 and B7, near the front.'

1 'Who acted Juliet?' 'I don't know. Check in the ....'

2 The .... must be ready for the dress rehearsal on Friday.

3 We're doing three .... of *Cinderella* – one on Friday and two on Saturday.

4 The play went well. Nobody forgot their ....

5 He's a brilliant actor. He always acts the .... in school plays.

6 The .... loved the pantomime. They laughed at all the jokes.

7 Milly plays the trumpet in the school ....

8 In opera, the story or .... isn't very important. The singing is more important.

9 At the end of the play we went on to the .... and danced with the actors.

10 I liked the party .... best. The costumes were great.

Grammar check

3 **Correct the mistake in each sentence.**
/\ = there's a word missing; X = change one word; ⤷ = change the order of two words; * = you must delete one word.

They just have left. ⤷
They have just left.

1 We've known him since three years. **X**

....

2 I already have had my breakfast. ⤷

....

3 He hasn't went to school yet. **X**

....

4 She's been here nine o'clock. /\

....

5 It's eight o'clock and he's already been gone to bed. *

....

....

4 **Circle the correct words for each sentence.**

... found his glasses yet?

A He has   **B** Did he   (**C** Has he)

1 Maria has worked there ... October.

A for   **B** since   **C** just

2 My sister ... bought a new scooter.

A just has   **B** has just   **C** did

3 We have had a dog ... a year.

A for   **B** since   **C** after

4 Louise ... at this school since 2003.

A has gone   **B** was   **C** has been

5 I've ... seen that film.

A already   **B** yet   **C** have

6 I haven't made the cake ...

A already   **B** yet   **C** just

7 I ... George for years.

A didn't see   **B** seen   **C** haven't seen

8 He has ... gone out.

A for   **B** last   **C** just

Extra!

1 Complete the sentences about Jack's trip to New York with the correct word. Circle A, B or C.

EXAMPLE

0 My friend Jack ...... New York last month.

A travelled   B visited   A went

1 He … in a hotel in the centre.

A stayed   B stood   C reserved

2 On the first day he … for a long walk around the city.

A took   B went   C turned

3 He got lost and couldn't … his hotel.

A find   B discover   C arrive

4 In the end, he asked someone the … .

A road   B path   C way

5 The man told him, 'You're right in … of your hotel!'

A middle   B side   C front

2 Match the clues to the travel words. There are two extra travel words.

EXAMPLE

0 You buy these to travel [H] on a bus, train or plane.

1 You go here to catch a plane.   [...]

2 It travels across the sea.   [...]

3 Only one or two people can travel on it. [...]

4 It's like a bus but it travels between towns. [...]

5 It can be a suitcase, a rucksack or a bag. [...]

A airport   D departure   G scooter

B bus stop   E ferry   H tickets

C coach   F luggage

EXAMPLE

0   Baggage reclaim   A   people at a gym
                            B   school children
                            C   tourists

1   Programmes £3   A   actors
                            B   the audience at a play
                            C   volunteers at an animal home

2   Italy 1 England 1   A   the audience at a play
                            B   people at a match
                            C   teachers

3   Don't forget the   A   students
        postcode!   B   people in a library
                            C   customers in a post office

4   Have you washed   A   workers in a kitchen
        your hands?   B   actors
                            C   football players

5   Please take   A   tourists
        your seats   B   teachers
                            C   the audience at a play

5 Complete the letters. Write ONE word for each space.

Dear Sam

How ..are.. you? I (1)................ got a bad cold so I'm
staying (2)............... bed today. Did you go (3)...............
Jen's party (4)............... night? I didn't because
I (5)............... n't well enough.

Love, Angie

Dear Angie

I (6)............... a great time at Jen's party. I'm sorry you
(7)............... n't well enough to go. But I'm (8)...............
a beach party (9)............... July 24th. I hope you
(10)............... come to it.

Love, Sam

4 Complete the dialogue. What does the customer say to the shop assistant? Choose from A–H. These are two extra responses.

> **EXAMPLE**
> **Shop assistant** Hello. Can I help you?
> **Customer** 0 ...F......

Shop assistant How long ago did you buy it?

Customer (1) ....

Shop assistant And what exactly is the problem?

Customer (2) ....

Shop assistant I'm sorry about that. I can give you another one, or you can have your money back.

Customer (3) ....

Shop assistant All right. Could you sign this form first, please.

Customer (4) ....

Shop assistant Thank you. Here's a new clock for you.

Customer (5) ....

Shop assistant I'm sure you won't have a problem this time. They're normally very good clocks.

A I never use a clock.
B I'd like to change it for another one, please.
C The alarm doesn't work. I was late for college this morning because it didn't wake me up.
D It was quite expensive. It cost £18.
E Just last week. It's still in its box.
F ~~Yes, please. I bought this alarm clock here and it doesn't work now.~~
G Thanks. Are you sure this one is going to work?
H Yes, of course.

6 You have to go out. Write a note to your friend, Zoe, who is staying with you. Say:
- **where you are going and why**
- **when you will be back**
- **what there is for her to do until you get back**
- **what she can eat and drink**
  Write 20–25 words.

....
....
....
....
....
....
....
....
....
....
....
....
....

GRAMMAR FILE

Zero conditional *if* clause

If you put water in the freezer, it becomes ice.
Water becomes ice if you put it in the freezer.
If you mix blue and yellow paint, you get green.
You get green if you mix blue and yellow paint.
If people don't sleep enough, they get ill.
People get ill if they don't sleep enough.
If you don't talk to them, babies don't learn to speak.
Babies don't learn to speak if you don't talk to them.
What happens if you put milk in the freezer?

- We use zero conditionals to talk about scientific facts, or things which are true, e.g. *If I eat a lot of chocolate, I get spots.* We also use zero conditionals to talk about logical consequences, e.g. *If one player hits the ball into the net, the other player gets a point.*
- We form zero conditional sentences with the Present simple in the *if* clause and in the main clause.
- We can often use *when* instead of *if* in zero conditionals, e.g. *If I eat a lot of chocolate, I get spots.* Or: *When I eat a lot of chocolate, I get spots.*

First conditional *if* clause

If it rains tomorrow, we'll stay at home.
We'll stay at home if it rains tomorrow.
If I don't do my homework now, I'll be in trouble tomorrow.
I'll be in trouble tomorrow if I don't do my homework now.
If you tell me the secret, I won't tell anyone else.
I won't tell anyone else if you tell me the secret.
If I don't dance with you, will you be annoyed?
Will you be annoyed if I don't dance with you?

- We use first conditionals to talk about something that is possible in the future.
- In first conditional sentences the verb in the *if* clause is in the Present simple and the verb in the main clause is in the future with *will,* e.g. *If you don't help me with my English, I won't lend you my new CD.*
- The main clause can also be an imperative or a question, e.g. *If the phone rings, don't answer it. What will you do if you can't find the address?*

If clause with *may* and *might*

If it's sunny tomorrow, we might go for a picnic.
If it's sunny tomorrow, we may go for a picnic.
We might go for a picnic if it's sunny tomorrow.
We may go for a picnic if it's sunny tomorrow.

- We can also use *may* or *might* + infinitive in the main clause of a first conditional. *May* and *might* mean the same thing – that something is possible but not certain, e.g. *If it's hot, we might go to the beach.* (= If it's hot, perhaps we will go).
- In all conditional sentences, we can put the *if* clause before or after the main clause. When the *if* clause comes first, there's a comma between it and the main clause, e.g. *If it rains, he drives to work. He drives to work if it rains. If I see her, I'll tell her. I'll tell her if I see her.*

Question tags

Affirmative sentence, negative tag

He's Australian, isn't he?

He's got a sister, hasn't he?

You live in Brighton, don't you?

He likes sport, doesn't he?

It was fun, wasn't it?

They were annoying, weren't they?

She won the tennis match, didn't she?

We've been to Wales, haven't we?

You can speak Russian, can't you?

The test will be quite easy, won't it?

Negative sentence, affirmative tag

She isn't usually late, is she?

She hasn't got a brother, has she?

You don't know my cousin Jo, do you?

She doesn't play football, does she?

It wasn't difficult, was it?

There weren't very many people, were there?

He didn't play very well, did he?

You haven't seen her, have you?

He can't play the piano, can he?

They won't be angry, will they?

- We use question tags to check information, e.g. *Jade's thirteen, isn't she? It isn't going to rain, is it?*
- With affirmative statements, we use a negative question tag, e.g. *You don't live in this street, do you?*
- With negative statements, we use an affirmative question tag, e.g. *She wasn't very angry with us, was she?*
- Question tags are in the same tense and person as the verb in the statement, e.g. *You've got a scooter, haven't you? Mina won't be at the party, will she? There wasn't any time, was there? You can swim, can't you? She doesn't like spiders, does she? He laughs a lot, doesn't he? You went to Brazil last year, didn't you?*
- With *I am* statements, the question tag is *aren't I*, e.g. *I'm the tallest, aren't I?*

Making polite requests

Do you mind if I open the window?

Is it all right if I call my dad?

May I take another biscuit?

- These three ways of asking to do something are all equally polite. How would you translate these three polite requests into your language?

  ....

  ....

  ....

5

Saturday morning on the farm

Vocabulary

1 **Find ten more animals in the word square.**

bull	cow	duck	~~goat~~	hen	sheep
cat	dog	fox	goose	horse	

S	H	S	B	G	O	T	A	O	G
H	P	O	L	B	C	A	O	T	C
E	E	O	L	W	W	C	D	O	W
N	E	G	U	X	F	H	O	E	N
D	H	E	B	F	O	X	G	C	A
C	S	G	O	O	S	E	Z	Y	E
K	C	U	D	M	Q	W	O	C	S
V	Y	Z	R	I	U	J	L	A	R
Q	J	C	A	T	M	I	P	M	O
G	O	R	D	H	S	E	C	A	H

2 **Match the words to the numbers.**

barn	......4......
cowshed	....
farmhouse	....
fence	....
field	....
gate	....
pond	....
stable	....
tree	....
yard	....

Dialogue work

3 **Complete the dialogue with the correct words.**

across	bull	cow	~~field~~	his	problem
banana	course	farmer	gates	know	

Eddie Come on. Let's go across this
field........... .

Becky The **(1)**...................... will be really angry
if he sees us.

Eddie No, he won't.

Becky How do you **(2)**..............?

Eddie Because my dad's the farmer and it's
(3).............. field.

Becky Oh.

Eddie Anyway, farmers only get angry if people
leave the **(4)** .... open. Come on.

Becky I still don't want to go **(5)**................ that
field.

Eddie What's the **(6)**............................ now?

Becky I'm scared of that **(7)**...............

Eddie That's a **(8)**.............., silly.

Becky Are you sure?

Eddie Of **(9)**................ I'm sure. Now come on.

Becky If it is a bull, what will we do?

Eddie Listen, Becky, if it's a bull, I'm a
(10)...........................

Grammar practice

4 **Match the sentence halves and complete the
sentences. Add a comma (,) where necessary.**

[.g] If it rains ...we have our PE lessons inside....

1 [...] Do bulls really get angry ....
....

2 [...] What do you do ....
....

3 [...] My mother gets worried ....
....

4 [...] If I drink coffee at night ....
....

5 [...] If my sister borrows my things ....
....

6 [...] In basketball you can't run ....
....

a) I can't sleep.
b) if I come home late.
c) if you can't sleep?
d) if you've got the ball.
e) if you wear something red?
f) she always loses them.
g) ~~we have our PE lessons inside.~~

5 **Put the words in order to make sentences.
Add a comma (,) where necessary.**

don't / miss / hurry / the / If / we'll / train / we
If we don't hurry, we'll miss the train,.........

1 all the / annoyed / be / cake / eat / if / Josie /
we / will
....
....

2 do / can't find / farm / if / the / What / we / we
/ will / ?
....
....

3 *Ghost Night* / films / If / like / love / scary / you /
you'll
....
....

4 a / doesn't / have / If / it / picnic / rain /
tomorrow / we'll
....
....

5 be / can / come / if / It / nice / on / really /
Saturday / will / you
....
....

6 a / buy / camera / enough / I / If / I'll / money /
save
....
....

5

6 Write sentences using *if* + Present simple in the first clause, and *might(n't)* + verb in the second clause.

you (sit) on that table / it (break)

If you sit on that table, it might break.

1 you (go) to the park now / you (find) Lily

....

....

2 the weather (be) nice tomorrow / we (have) a barbecue

....

....

3 I (have) enough money by July / I (buy) a camera

....

....

4 Kate (not do) some work this term / she (not pass) her exams

....

....

5 you (not shut) the gate / the sheep (get) out

....

....

6 I (not go) to football practice today / Josh (not let) me be in the match on Saturday

....

....

....

7 we (sit) in the garden / we (not hear) the phone

....

....

8 you (not write) this down / you (not remember) it

....

....

7 Write sentences in the first conditional using the verbs in (brackets).

We 'll _be_....... late if we _don't go_. now. (be / not go)

1 If you .... another cup of coffee, you .... tonight. (have / not sleep)

2 If you .... to bed now, you ....tired in the morning (not go / be)

3 There .... any breakfast if Eddie .... the eggs. (not be / not collect)

4 If our cat .... kittens, we .... one to you. (have / give)

5 I .... upset if Jamie .... my birthday again. (be / forget)

6 If we .... across the field, it .... quicker. (walk / be)

7 I .... you if you .... a party tomorrow. (help / have)

8 If Naomi .... soon, we .... without her. (not arrive / go)

8 Complete the questions with the correct tag.

You live in Cambridge, _don't you?_.....................?

1 Anna made this cake, ...?

2 Ben's at your school, ...?

3 It'll be cold later, ...?

4 It's hot, ...?

5 Lucy was angry, ...?

6 She's got blonde hair, ...?

7 You're Australian, ...?

8 Steve speaks Spanish, ...?

9 The hens were hungry, ...?

10 We can go across this field, ...?

11 You've got a rabbit, ...?

12 There was a terrible storm, ...?

13 Your dad has been to China, ...?

9 **Complete the questions with the correct tag.**

You don't eat meat, ...do you...........................?

1 Adam hasn't got a brother, ...?

2 You won't tell Mum, ...?

3 I wasn't going very fast, ...?

4 Maria hasn't written, ...?

5 You can't ride a horse, ...?

6 Pippo doesn't like fish, ...?

7 You weren't listening, ...?

8 The party wasn't very good, ...?

9 There weren't many people there, ...?

10 You aren't annoyed, ...?

11 They didn't enjoy the play, ...?

12 You haven't got a scooter, ...?

13 This isn't your puppy, ...?

14 Your parents haven't left yet, ...?

10 **Match the sentence halves. Write the complete sentences adding question tags.**

[e.] Penguins can't fly, can they?...........

1 [...] Frankfurt isn't ....
....

2 [...] Marilyn Monroe was ....
....

3 [...] Marconi invented ....
....

4 [...] Spiders have got ....
....

5 [...] A lot of coffee comes ....
....

6 [...] There aren't any ....
....

7 [...] VOLLEYBALL has got ....
....

8 [...] Juan is ....
....

9 [...] Most cats don't ....
....

10 [...] Shakespeare wrote ....

a) a Spanish name
b) an American film star
c) from Brazil
d) eight legs
e) ~~fly~~
f) four Ls in it
g) plays
h) swim
i) the capital of Germany
j) the radio
k) tigers in Africa

11 **Make polite requests for each picture using one of these phrases.**

Do you mind if ...   Is it all right if ...   May I ...

Is it all right if I turn the light on?

1 ....
....
....

2 ....
....
....

3 ....
....
....

4 ....
....
....

5 ....
....
....

Skills development

Blind people might soon start using ponies instead of dogs as guides. In America, Cuddles, the world's first guide pony, started working in May this year. She has already got on and off planes with her owner, Dan Shaw, and gone up and down escalators at airports. Cuddles, a miniature pony, is only fifty-two centimetres high and is very calm. She is not frightened of traffic and doesn't panic on busy streets. Dan Shaw, who has been blind for twenty-seven years, says, 'Cuddles is part of my family now.' Janet Burleson, Cuddles's, trainer is also very pleased with Cuddles. She says, 'You can train a horse to do anything a dog can do'.

Cuddles understands 23 commands, including "wait" and "forward". And she is very clean. If she needs to go outside for the toilet, she stamps her foot!'

There are a lot of good reasons to use miniature horses as guides for the blind. Horses have an instinct to guide. If a wild horse goes blind, another horse will often look after it.

And if a rider hurts himself, his horse will often carry him safely home. Miniature ponies live 30 to 40 years. Guide dogs can only work for about 12 years. It's also cheaper to train a guide pony. It costs £35,000 to train a guide dog and only £10,000 to train a guide pony. Horses have excellent memories. They don't forget dangerous situations and they always look for the safest routes. Horses are healthy and strong and don't get tired if they have to travel a long way. They also have excellent eyes and can see in the dark. Horses do not try to get attention from humans all the time like dogs.

Some people say horses are more nervous than dogs. 'If a horse gets frightened, it wants to run away,' says Patrick Mactaggart, a professional dog trainer. 'I think dogs will always be the best guides for the blind.' But Dan Shaw doesn't agree. 'I've always loved horses,' he says. 'I never expected to own one. And I never expected it to be my eyes.'

Read

1 **Read the text and tick (✓) the best title for it.**

1 [...] Guide Dogs Are Best

2 [...] A Very Expensive Animal

3 [...] **Ponies help the blind**

4 [...] Blind For 27 Years

5 [...] A Very Clever Dog

6 [...] A Dangerous Job

2 Write T (true) or F (false).

1 Cuddles has been on a plane. ..F...
2 Cuddles is a large horse. ......
3 Cuddles is frightened of cars. ......
4 Horses often help their riders. ......
5 Ponies only live about 12 years. ......
6 Ponies are more expensive to train
than dogs. ......
7 Horses remember a lot. ......
8 Horses can see in the dark. ......

Write

3 Imagine you saw Dan Shaw and Cuddles in your town. Write a letter to a friend about them. Use information in the article and your imagination. Use these notes to help you.

Dear ....,

Last week I was in/at ....
when I saw a blind man with a guide pony. I was
really surprised. The pony was (describe the pony.)

....

....

It helped the man to ....

....

....

When the man wanted to ....

...., the pony

....

The pony could ....

....

I've seen a guide dog but I've never seen a guide

pony. What about you?

Love from ....

Study tips

4 When you read or listen in your own language, you can often guess the ending of the sentence. Try to guess the endings of these sentences. There are no right or wrong answers.

1 I fell out of the boat into the river and lost my
....

2 He didn't go to the gym because he couldn't find
....

3 The workers took the bananas off the boat and
put them in ....

4 She chose the grey kitten because it was
....

5 She wanted to be a vet because she loved
....

6 He wrote a long letter to her but he didn't post it
because he didn't have ....

5 Becky is talking about horse riding. Guess the ending of each sentence.

1 I love horses and I'm quite good at ....
2 Unfortunately I don't have my own ....
3 And of course riding is very ....
4 I don't get enough pocket money to pay for
....
5 Last year I got a Saturday job in a stable near
....
6 I go there every Saturday afternoon for about
....
7 I brush the ....
8 I also give them ..their...................................
9 The longest job is cleaning the ....
10 The owners don't ....
11 But I get a free ride at the end of....................

5 Talk time

1 **Write the phrases in the correct balloons.**

- Don't worry.
- for ages
- I wish I could go.
- Just one thing,
- much later
- Never mind

They're going fishing again.
....
....

I've forgotten my swimming goggles.

....
I've got two pairs.

Hurry! The train leaves in six hours.

....
We'll be there in time.

I haven't been skating
....

have you passed your driving test?

I got up at eleven this morning. How about you?

I got up ....
- around two in the afternoon!

2 **Complete the dialogues with these words.**

all   course   fine   Go   ~~May~~   mind   right   Would

A May I use your phone?

B Yes, of (1)..........................

A (2) .... you like a drink?

B No, thank you.

A Do you (3)..................... if I close the window?

B Not at (4)............. . (5)..................... ahead.

A I'll call you tomorrow, if that's all (6)...................

B Yes, that'll be (7)...................

Let's check

Vocabulary check

1 Put the letters in order to make animal words.

act   ..cat..............

1 lubl   ....

2 woc   ....

3 shore   ....

4 knodey   ....

5 heeps   ....

6 toga   ....

7 cukd   ....

8 sogoe   ....

9 tenkit   ....

10 yuppp   ....

2 Match the animals to the places where they are kept.

hens	[e]	a)	stable
1 sheep	[...]	b)	field
2 cows	[...]	c)	pond
3 ducks	[...]	d)	cowshed
4 horses	[...]	e)	~~yard~~

Grammar check

3 Correct the mistakes in each sentence.
/\ = there's a word missing; X = change one word; ↪ = change the order of two words; * = you must delete one word.

You went to a party last week, hadn't you? **X**

..You.went.to.a.party.last.week,.didn't.you?........

1 If you run, you might to find her at the bus stop. *

....
....

2 Do you mind I borrow your pen for a minute? /\

....
....

3 If you will write to her, please give her my love. *

....
....

4 I may have another glass of water? ↪

....
....

4 Circle the correct words for each sentence.

She hasn't eaten all the crisps, ...?

A was she   (**B** has she)   **C** did she

1 If I ... him, I'll tell you.

A see   **B** will see   **C** saw

2 If you give me her address, I might ... to her.

A to write   **B** write   **C** writing

3 She's got dark hair, ...?

A hasn't she   **B** isn't it   **C** isn't she

4 Do you mind ... I turn the light on?

A if   **B** that   **C** for

5 If Jodie is late again, ... wait for her.

A I won't   **B** I wasn't   **C** I'll be

6 The kittens didn't want their food, ...?

A were they   **B** did they   **C** didn't they

7 You've shut the gate, ...?

A haven't you   **B** didn't you   **C** hasn't it

8 You won't tell anyone, ... you?

A do   **B** can   **C** will

9 You haven't been to Turkey, ... you?

A did   **B** have   **C** were

10 If you know her name, please ... me.

A telling   **B** told   **C** tell

5 Make sentences by putting the words in order.

I / if / Do / mind / open / the / window / you / ?

..Do.you.mind.if.I.open.the.window?..................

1 coach / won't leave / The / us, / will it / without / ?

....
....

2 to collect / do it / If you don't / the eggs, / have time / I'll

....
....

3 can I / the car, / extra / have / If I / money / pocket / some / wash / ?

....
....

GRAMMAR FILE

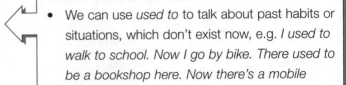

used to

Affirmative

I used to hate sport (but now I like it).
You used to have long hair (but now it's short).
She used to be in my class (but now she isn't).
It used to be a shoe shop (but now it's a phone shop).
We used to wear school uniform (but now we don't).
They used to live in a village (but now they live in a town).

Negative

I didn't use to walk to school (but now I do).
You didn't use to walk to school (but now you do).
He didn't use to walk to school (but now he does).
We didn't use to walk to school (but now we do).
They didn't use to walk to school (but now they do).

Questions

Did I use to live in a village?
Did you use to live in a village?
Did he / she use to live in a village?
Did we use to live in a village?
Did they use to live in a village?

Short answers
Affirmative

Yes, I / you / he / she / we / they did.

Negative

No, I / you / he / she / we / they didn't.

Wh? questions

When did I use to have breakfast?
Where did you use to live?
Why did she use to fight with Jo?
How did we use to get to school?
What did they use to watch on TV?

- We can use *used to* to talk about past habits or situations, which don't exist now, e.g. *I used to walk to school. Now I go by bike. There used to be a bookshop here. Now there's a mobile phone shop.*
- The negative is *didn't use to*, e.g. *She didn't use to like sport. Now she plays tennis every day. The desk didn't use to be here. It used to be next to the window.*
- The question form is *did ... use to ...?* e.g. *Did you use to wear school uniform at your last school? Where did your mother use to work?*

Adjectives followed by *to* + infinitive

It's easy to make pancakes.
Sometimes it's hard to understand.
I think it's interesting to look at the stars.
It's boring to play computer games all day.
It's always nice to make new friends.
It's dangerous to play football on the road.
You know it's bad to tell lies.
We were sorry to leave.

- We often use an adjective + infinitive (with *to*) to express our opinions. Here are some further examples.
  It's often difficult to remember new words.
  It's not safe to cross the road now.
  It's silly to talk in class.
  It's great to see you again!
  It's impossible to swim 200 metres under water.
  It was good to get your postcard.
  It's very exciting to ski down mountains.

The infinitive of purpose

I'm going to the shops to buy some bread and milk.
Do you use a computer to do your homework?
He stayed up late to watch the match on TV.
Can you go to the post office to post these letters?

- We can use *to* with the infinitive to say why someone does something, e.g. *I'm phoning to tell you about my party. They broke the window to get into the house.*

Verbs followed by *to* + infinitive

I want to take some photos at the concert.
Would you like to go to the beach?
She hopes to go to university in America.
They're planning to go out tonight.
We didn't expect to see you here.
What do you need to get at the shops?
They're learning to windsurf.
You should try to get there early.

- Some verbs are followed by *to* + infinitive. Here is a list of some of them:

expect	need	want
hope	plan	would like
learn	try	

Verbs followed by the gerund

He really enjoys meeting new people.
I don't mind waiting a few minutes.
I'm looking forward to seeing you again.
I must finish doing my homework first.
Do you fancy going to the cinema tonight?
She gave up eating chocolate for a year.
Sometimes I can't help laughing at my brother.

- Some verbs are followed by the gerund (*-ing* form). Here is a list of some of them:

can't/couldn't help	give up
enjoy	look forward to
fancy	(not) mind
finish	

Verbs followed by the infinitive or the gerund

Andy likes going out with his friends.
I don't like to stay in on Saturday evening.
Do you prefer swimming in pools or in the sea?
I prefer to swim in the sea.
She started to sing. Then everyone started singing.
I hate being late. But I also hate to arrive before everyone else.

- Some verbs can be followed by *to* + infinitive or the gerund (*-ing* form). Here is a list of some of them:

like	hate	start
love	prefer	

- We use *to* + infinitive after *would like, would love, would hate, would prefer*, NOT the gerund.
  I'd like to go swimming on Sunday.
  Josie would prefer to go to the beach too.
  NOT: ~~I'd like going swimming on Sunday.~~
  ~~Josie would prefer going to the beach too.~~

6

It's great to be outside

Vocabulary

1 **What are the jobs? Put the letters in the right order.**
Then match the jobs to the pictures.

C H A R I T T E C		M A R R E F

a rchitect.......... [d]

3 .... [...]

F E C H

1 .... [...]

R I F E

T H I G E R F

S T I N T E D

4 f........................

2 .... [...]

f........................ [...]

T H L I G F

D A T T E N T A N

5 f........................

a .... [...]

H A R I R E D S E R S

6 h.........d............ [...]

R O J U N S T I L A

7 j........................ [...]

a)

b)

c)

d)

e)

f)

g)

h)

i)

j)

k)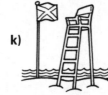

l)

m)

n)

o)

F I L E D R A U G

8 l..........g............ [...]

S U R N E

9 .... [...]

P O O R H A T P H E R G

10 p........................ [...]

C O R K

C U S M I A N I

11 r........................

m........................ [...]

S E A L S

S A S S I T T N A

12 s ....

a .... [...]

T I S T N I C E S

13 s .... [...]

O Z O

P E R K E E

14 z ....

k .... [...]

Dialogue work

2 **Complete the dialogue with the correct words.**

grandma	frightened	try
lovely	poor	mind
~~arm~~	money	joking

Becky   Watch out. There's a really big spider on your ...arm..... .

Rachel Where? I can't see one.

Becky   Only (1)...…......……….. I said it to scare you.

Rachel Well, you didn't scare me.

Becky   Too bad! You used to be (2)...............…......... of spiders.

Rachel I used to be, but I don't (3)...…........... them now.

Becky   My (4)..........…........ says spiders are lucky.

Rachel Lucky?

Becky   She says if a spider walks across your hand, you get (5)...…...........

Rachel Really?

Becky   Yes. You should (6)...….......... it some time. Think of all that (7)..…........... money!

Rachel It's OK, thanks. I prefer being (8)...…...........

Grammar practice

3 **When the Gardner Family moved from London to a seaside village, their son Nick's life changed a lot.**

a) Write sentences with *He used to...* .

He lived in a flat on a busy street.

1 He took the bus to school.

2 He played football on Wednesdays.

3 He wore school uniform.

4 He spent all his free time skateboarding.

He used to live in a flat on a busy street.

1 ....

....

2 ....

....

3 ....

....

4 ....

....

b) Write sentences with *He didn't use to...* .

Now he lives in a big house with a garden.

5 He cycles to school.

6 He does athletics on Wednesdays.

7 He wears jeans to school.

8 He spends all his free time surfing.

He didn't use to live in a big house with a garden.

5 ....

....

6 ....

....

7 ....

....

8 ....

4 **Write sentences with *used to/didn't use to* and the Present or Past simple.**

I didn't use to like. (not like) coffee but now I drink. (drink) it every day.

Alice didn't use to have.(not have) a dog but she got. (get) one last year.

1 Mark ....…..........(have) a scooter but he ....(sell) it last week.

2 Kirsty ....… (not do) sport but now she ....(play) tennis every week.

3 Jamie ....(live) in York but he .... (move) to Leeds two years ago.

4 We .... (not like) each other but we .... (be) friends now.

5 People .... (write) a lot of letters but now they .... (send) e-mails.

6 You .... (fight) with your brother but now you .... (fight) with your sister.

7 There .... (be) a swimming pool here but they .... (close) it last year.

8 I .... (go) to school by bus but now my mother ....…... (take) me in the car.

5 Read the text then write the interviewer's questions, using a verb from the box with *use to* or the Present simple.

| buy | get | go | live | ~~work~~ |

THE MILLIONAIRE STUDENT

Two years ago, 25-year-old Fern Donovan was a sales assistant in a shoe shop. Then she won £10 million and her life changed completely. Fern told us 'I'm still the same person but I don't have to worry about money now.'

Where did you use to work? ....

In a shoe shop.

Where do you work now? ....

I don't work. I'm at college again. I'm studying languages.

1 ....?

I shared a very small, dark flat with two other girls.

2 ....?

I've got a beautiful house with a pool in Chelsea.

3 ....to work?

I used to cycle.

4 ....to college now?

I drive there in my Porsche.

5 ....
.... for your holidays?

I used to go camping in Dorset.

6 ....for your holidays now?

To the Caribbean, Thailand, the Seychelles.

7 ....
.... your clothes?

I didn't buy any new clothes. My cousins gave me their old clothes.

8 ....your clothes now?

Gucci, Valentino, Versace! Money isn't a problem!

6 Complete the captions with the correct phrases.

- cross this road
- go down
- learn a new language
- ~~run across roads~~
- sleep all day
- put your head in the sand
- swim in the rain

It's..... dangerous to run across....... roads...................

1 .... difficult
....
....
....

2 .... easy
....
....
....

3 .... fun
....
....
....

4 .... boring
....
....
....

5 .... silly
....
....
....

6 .... impossible
....
....
....

7 Write eight sentences giving your opinion about the activities on the right.

boring	dangerous	difficult
embarrassing	fun	great
important	impossible	silly

It's important to...... do sport every week.

1 .... be good at music.

2 .... stay in bed all day.

3 .... surf the internet.

4 .... learn about different countries.

5 .... climb trees.

6 .... forget your lines in a play

7 .... fight with people.

8 Match the sentence halves using an infinitive of purpose.

[f.] We're staying at home
   to watch the big match. ....

1 [...] I'm going to the post office

   ....

2 [...] He's gone to the café

   ....

3 [...] Are you using the computer

   ....

4 [...] I've bought some tomatoes

   ....

5 [...] Do you want to come to the park

   ....

6 [...] Did you ring Maria

   ....

a) ask about the rehearsal   e) play football
b) buy some stamps   f) watch the big match
c) have a drink with Jo   g) write your project
d) make a pasta sauce

9 Write four sentences giving your opinion of certain activities.

I think it's dangerous to play with fire. ......

1 ....dangerous ....

   ....

2 ....silly..................................

   ....

3 ....fun ....

   ....

4 ....easy ....

   ....

10 Complete the sentences putting the verbs into the correct form.

I don't like ..living.. (live) here. I'd prefer to live. (live) by the sea.

1 She doesn't enjoy .... (be) the centre of attention.

2 Would you like ....,.............(get) a job as a TV presenter?

3 She plans .... (spend) the summer working on a farm.

4 Andy's learning .... (surf) this summer.

5 I don't mind .... (stay) in this evening.

6 I didn't expect .... (see) you here.

7 I prefer .... (swim) to .... (lie) in the sun.

8 We must try .... (meet) before the holidays.

9 I really hate .... (get) up early.

10 You don't need .... (bring) any food to the picnic.

11 Do you fancy .... (go) for a walk by the river?

Culture spot

A Cotswold Village

A Cotswold Village by Hannah Colwell   Year 8

I live in a **sleepy** village called Stanton. Stanton is in the Cotswolds – a range of hills in the west of England. There used to be lots of sheep farms here and the Cotswolds used to be the centre of the **wool** industry. These days a lot of old people come to live here when they **retire**. Nothing happens in Stanton and the village hasn't changed for about 300 years. In fact, film companies often come here to make films about the eighteenth century. There's one **pub**. Everyone goes there for a drink on Sunday mornings, but that's it. There isn't a cinema, a sports centre, a café or a **petrol station** – in fact, there isn't even a village shop. So it isn't difficult to make a film about the past in Stanton because there is nothing modern except the bus stop.

We have a beautiful old house that's nearly 400 years old. Like a lot of houses in the Cotswolds, it's got yellow **stone** walls and a pretty garden. I've got my own horse and I really enjoy riding around the countryside with my best friend Charlotte. Another thing that's really fun in Stanton is **tobogganing** down the hill when it snows.

When Mum's friend from London visits us, she always talks about the beautiful countryside and perfect villages of the Cotswolds. She thinks we're really lucky to live here 'in all this **fresh air**'! But life here isn't perfect. There isn't even a school in Stanton. My mum used to drive me to the primary school in Didbrook, the next village. Now I'm at secondary school in Winchcombe, which is 8 kilometres away. Luckily there's a school bus to take me there. Winchcombe is quite a lot bigger than Stanton. There are actually some shops there, several cafés and some other kids my age!

My big problem here in Stanton is **public transport**. There are buses but there aren't enough. In the summer I sometimes cycle to Winchcombe but I don't like cycling in the winter. If I want to go to Cheltenham – the nearest town, I usually ask my parents to drive me. It's about half an hour away by car. I can't wait to be seventeen and pass my **driving test**!

1 **Read the text and answer the questions.**

1 What are the Cotswolds?

....

2 Why is it easy to make films about the eighteenth century in Stanton?

....

3 How old is Hannah's house?

....

4 What does Hannah like doing with Charlotte?

....

5 How did she use to get to primary school?

....

6 Why is Hannah looking forward to her seventeenth birthday?

....

2 **Match the captions to the photos.**

a) I've got my own horse.

b) There are no shops but there's one pub in the village.

c) the cars are modern but nothing else is in Stanton.

d) We have a great time here when it snows!

[...] 1

[...] 2

[...] 3

[...] 4

Vocabulary

3 **Guess the meaning of these words and write a translation. Then check in a dictionary.**

sleepy ....

wool ....

retire ....

pub ....

petrol station ....

stone ....

tobogganing ....

fresh air ....

public transport ....

driving test ....

Portfolio

4 **Describe your ideal place to live.**

I'd like to live in a (*type of house/flat, etc.*)
....

with a (*garden? roof garden? balcony? swimming pool?*) ....
....

in (*name of city/town/village/country*) ....
....

I'd like a (*describe your ideal room*) ....
....

with a view of (*describe your ideal view*) ....
....
....

I'd like to have a (*name something you'd like to own*)
....
....

I'd like to live near a (*finish this sentence*)...............
....

Let's read

When I leave school ...

1 **Put the dialogue in the correct order. Number the sentences 1–6.**

[...] Because I'd like to travel all round the world and take photos of interesting places.

[...] Yes. What job would you like to have?

[...] I'd like to be a photographer.

[...] What are you going to be?

[...] Why?

[...] Do you mean when I leave school?

2 **Read what five teenagers say about future studies and jobs. Then read the questions (a–g) and write the correct letters in the boxes.**

Who ...

a) wants to work with animals?

b) would like to work for a television company?

c) is interested in science?

d) wants to be famous?

e) is really interested in food?

f) wants to study more but hasn't decided on a career?

g) comes from an international family?

Claudia [.b.]
I'd like to be a TV presenter or a journalist for TV news. But it's not easy to get that kind of work.

Alex [...]
I haven't thought about a job yet. I don't know what kind of work to do. But I'd like to go to university when I leave school.

Natasha [...]
My parents want me to be an interpreter because I already speak three languages. You see, my mum's Russian and my dad's German and we live in England. So they think it's the obvious job for me.

Sabina [...]
I'd like to be a rock star. It probably won't happen but it's fun to dream!

Will [...]
I'm going to be a vet. I've always wanted to be a vet. I decided that when I was five. It's the only job for me.

Eleanor [...]
I'd like to work in a laboratory. But I don't want to do experiments on animals.

Andy [...]
I don't want to go to university. I'd like to start training as a chef when I leave school. I love cooking and everyone says I'm good at it.

Let's check

Vocabulary check

1 Reorder the letters to find the answers.

CHATRITEC	FECH	RETERPRETIN
FELIDRAGU	TEV	STURNOJALI
YOCKEJ	~~RUSEN~~	THLIGF TADNTANET
HARISERSERD		LEASS TISSANSTA

Who …

works in a hospital? ...NURSE..........................

1 cuts hair? ....

2 cooks? ....

3 must be a good rider?..............................

4 works with animals? ....

5 designs buildings?...................................

6 works in a shop?......................................

7 writes for newspapers? ....

8 speaks lots of languages?........................

9 must be an excellent swimmer? ....

10 works on a plane?....................................

Grammar check

2 Correct the mistake in each sentence.
/\ = there's a word missing; X = change one
word; ↪ = change the order of two words;
*** = you must delete one word.**

We're going to the park meet Joanna. /\
We're going to the park to meet Joanna..........

1 I didn't used to like swimming. **X**

....

2 We're staying in for to watch TV. *****

....

3 I learnt swim when I was three. **/**

....

....

4 Where you did use to go to school? ↪

....

....

3 Circle the correct words for each sentence.

She … live near us.

  A use   **B** use to   (**C** used to)

1 I don't mind … my room.

  A for tidying **B** tidy **C** tidying

2 I used to … a sweet little dog.

  A had   **B** have   **C** having

3 It's really fun … swimming at night.

  A to go **B** go **C** for go

4 He's gone to the shops … for some new
trainers.

  A to look **B** for looking **C** for to look

5 It's impossible … fast up this hill.

  A cycling **B** cycle **C** to cycle

6 Did your mother … to be a flight attendant?

  A use   **B** used   **C** using

7 I'm staying up late … The World Cup on TV.

  A for watch **B** to watch **C** for watching

8 Did she hate … in the school concert?

  A singing **B** she sings **C** sing

9 She still hasn't finished … her room.

  A paint **B** painting **C** to paint

10 My brother is hoping … famous one day!

  A be   **B** being   **C** to be

4 Make sentences by putting the words in
order.

enjoy / I / meeting / new / people / really
I really enjoy meeting new people................

1 and chocolate / eating / given up / I've / sweets

....

....

2 at / exciting / It's / look / stars / the / to

....

....

3 a / Did / farm / have / horse / to / use / you /
on your / ?

....

....

1 **Read the text and answer the questions.**

Edison – the world's greatest inventor

Thomas Alva Edison was born in 1847 in Milan, Ohio. He was one of seven children. He first went to school at the age of eight, but he didn't do very well. The teacher didn't realise that he was slightly deaf, and thought he was stupid. In fact, the teacher told Edison he was stupid, and the poor boy ran home crying to his mother. He went back to school from time to time until the age of twelve, but received most of his education from his mother. He also taught himself a lot – he was a keen reader of science books.

As soon as he left school, he got a job selling newspapers on the street. He immediately showed his intelligence and business sense in the job. Each day, he read the news stories before he took the newspapers from the shop. When they were interesting, he picked up a lot of papers – when they were less interesting, he picked up a smaller number. With this simple trick, he made much more money than the other newspaper boys.

Edison's first invention appeared when he was only nineteen. He then started work as a full-time inventor, creating new machines or improving machines which already existed. For example, Alexander Graham Bell had invented the telephone in 1876, but Edison made a new and much better microphone for it.

In 1877 Edison produced the first sound-recording machine called the phonograph. Without that essential first step, we would not have any cassettes or CDs today – so spare Edison a thought the next time you listen to your favourite album! Two years later, he invented the light bulb. New York became the first city in the world with electric lighting.

In the late 1880s he produced a movie camera and projector – the kinetograph and the kinetoscope. So he was also one of the fathers of the film industry. At the same time, he invented electrical batteries for use with his new cameras.

Altogether, more than 1,000 inventions came out of Edison's laboratory. When he died in 1931, the lights were switched off all over the USA as a tribute.

1 How many brothers and sisters did Edison have?

2 Why did he run home from school?

3 At what age did he leave school?

4 Who was his best teacher?

5 How old was Edison when he started inventing?

6 How did he improve the telephone?

7 What was the phonograph?

8 In which year did he invent the light bulb?

9 What did Edison do for the film industry?

10 How many things did Edison invent?

11 Which of his inventions do you think was the most important? Why?

12 What would you most like to invent yourself?

Answers

1 ....

2 ....
   ....

3 ....

4 ....
   ....

5 ....

6 ....
   ....

7 ....
   ....

8 ....

9 ....
   ....

10 ....

11 ....
    ....
    ....

12 ....
    ....

Letter writing

 2 **Write a letter to your pen-friend describing a bad day.**

- First think of the occasion. Were you late for something? Did you lose something? Did you have an accident? Did you have a fight with a friend or member of your family? Did you get into trouble at school?

- When did it happen? Where were you? Who were you with?

- What were you doing when things started to go wrong? *I was ...ing when ....*

- Describe what happened. Use the Past continuous and Past simple. For example: *I woke up late. I ate breakfast fast. I was running for the bus when I dropped my ...*

- How did you feel? Was anyone sympathetic and kind to you?

- Show you have finished talking about your bad day with a phrase like *I'm glad that day is over now. / I never want to have another day like that.*

- Sign your letter.

Write between 100 and 120 words.

Dear ....

....

....

....

....

....

....

....

....

....

....

....

....

....

....

Please write to me soon. ....

Best wishes ....

GRAMMAR FILE

Subject relative pronouns: *who, which, that*

I know the girl who was on TV last night.
He's getting a camera which costs £300.
He's getting a camera that costs £300.

- We can use the relative pronouns *who, which, that* to join two clauses.
- We use *who* for people, e.g. *I have a friend. He stands on his head every day. = I have a friend who stands on his head every day.*
- We use *which* or *that* for things and animals, e.g. *She's got a cat. It watches television. = She's got a cat which watches television.* Or: *She's got a cat that watches television.*

Object relative pronouns: *who, which, that*

What's the name of the girl who we saw in the park?
He's lending me the CD which he bought last week.
He's lending me the CD that he bought last week.
What the name of the girl we saw in the park?
He's lending me the CD he bought last week.

- We can leave out the object relative pronouns *who, which, that* in speaking and writing: *Do you remember the boy? We met him in Scotland. = Do you remember the boy who we met in Scotland?* Or: *Do you remember the boy we met in Scotland? Do you like the book? I bought it for you. = Do you like the book that I bought for you?* Or: *Do you like the book which I bought for you?* Or: *Do you like the book I bought for you?*

- In formal English, we can use the object relative clause *whom* instead of *who* but it is not common in spoken English, e.g. *The boy whom they met in Scotland was very helpful.*

Relative pronouns: *where, whose*

We never go to that beach where you can rent canoes.
Let's go to that café where you can get really cheap ice creams.
I have a friend whose brother is a racing driver.
Do you remember that girl whose mother is a TV presenter?

- We use the relative pronoun *where* for places, e.g. *Let's go to the field. We had the picnic there = Let's go to the field where we had the picnic.*
- We use the relative pronoun *whose* for possession, e.g. *What's the name of the girl? You borrowed her jacket. = What's the name of the girl whose jacket you borrowed?*

Present simple passive

Affirmative

I'm expected to help with the washing up.

You're sometimes driven to school.

Jack is often taken to concerts.

Tea is grown in China and India.

We are given a lot of homework.

A lot of oranges are grown in Spain and Morocco.

The doors are locked at seven o'clock.

Negative

I'm not expected to help with the cooking.

You aren't allowed to cycle to school.

Abby isn't taken to football matches.

Tea isn't grown in Europe.

We aren't allowed to eat in class.

Oranges aren't grown in Scotland.

These rooms aren't cleaned very often.

Questions

Am I expected to do this today?

Are you allowed to go out during the week?

Is Jade allowed to have parties at her house?

Where is coffee grown?

Is it grown in South America?

Why are we given homework every day?

Where are the keys kept?

Are these doors locked every night?

- We often use the passive to stress the action rather than the person who does it, e.g. *The swimming pool is cleaned once a week. The toilets are cleaned every day.*

- We also use the passive to give formal information about rules, e.g. *Dinner is served at eight o'clock. The doors are locked every night. Cycles are not allowed in this park.*

- To make the Present simple passive, we use the present tense of the verb *be* and the past participle of the main verb, e.g. *Coffee is grown in Guatemala. Some of the best chocolates are made in Belgium. I'm not allowed to stay out late during the week. When are these gates locked? How long are you expected to spend on your homework?*

- We use *by* to say who an action is done by, e.g. *The hamster cage is cleaned every day by my brother. The bins are emptied every day by the cleaners.*

The girl who lives in Mexico City

Vocabulary

1 **Match the words to the numbers.**

blind 13

coffee machine ....

cooker ....

cushion...

dishwasher ....

freezer ....

fridge ....

kettle ....

microwave ....

music system ....

oven ....

sink ....

sofa ....

tap ....

toaster ....

washing machine ....

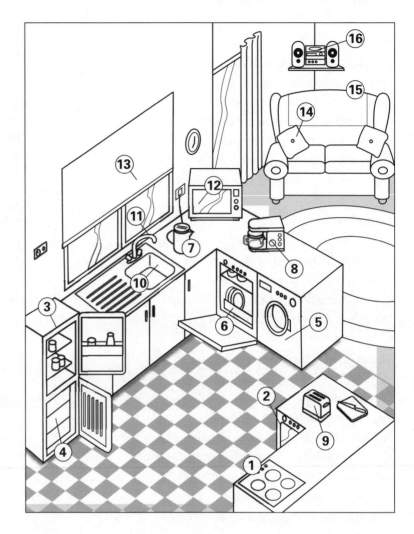

Dialogue work

2 **Complete the dialogue with the sentences.**

Guest	I'd like to book a room for two nights, please.
Receptionist	Would you like a single room or a double?
Guest	(1) ....
Receptionist	For how many nights?
Guest	(2) ....
Receptionist	When is this for?
Guest	(3) ....
Receptionist	A double room with bathroom is £80 per night.
Guest	(4) ....

Receptionist	Yes, it is.
Guest	(5) ....
Receptionist	I'm afraid pets aren't allowed in this hotel.
Guest	(6) ....
Receptionist	I'm very sorry. Animals are not allowed in any part of the hotel.

- Is breakfast included?
- It's only a little dog. And he's always very good.
- I'd like a double room, with a bathroom.
- ~~I'd like to book a room for two nights, please.~~
- Is it OK to bring my dog?
- The 23rd and 24th May. How much will it be?
- Two.

Grammar practice

3 **Join the sentences using *who* or *which*.**

Smash is a new magazine. It has articles and stories about musicians.

Smash is a new magazine which has articles and stories about musicians.

1 Davina McCall is a TV presenter. She got famous with *Big Brother*.

....
....

2 *Endz* is a new computer game. It makes you think.

....
....

3 *The Lola 230* is a mobile phone. It can send photos.

....
....

4 *City Tours* has wonderful tour guides. They really know London.

....
....

5 *Fizzit* is a new drink. It's good for your teeth.

....
....

6 *Sky Air* has great flight attendants. They will always help you.

....
....

7 *Beach* is a new perfume. It smells of the sea.

....
....

8 Patrick Swayze is a dancer. He starred in *Dirty Dancing*.

....
....

4 **Complete the sentences with *who* or *which*.**

I know a girl .....who..... lives on a houseboat.

1 Do you like films .... make you laugh?

2 The people .... live in that house own a racehorse.

3 Do you remember the people .... used to live next door?

4 She bought a pair of trainers .... cost £100.

5 A jockey is a person .... rides horses in races.

6 There's a shop opposite my house .... sells really cheap CDs.

7 A vegetarian is a person .... doesn't eat meat.

8 Animals .... eat meat are called carnivores.

5 **Complete the sentences with *whose* or *where*.**

We usually go to a beach .where... you can do waterskiing.

1 There's a boy in my class .... mother is a TV presenter.

2 Let's go to a café .... you can sit outside.

3 Do you know that cinema .... you can get really cheap popcorn?

4 I've got really small feet. I don't know anybody .... shoes fit me.

5 A place .... you keep horses is a stable.

6 I know someone .... brother was in the Olympic Games.

We can use *that* or *which* when we give information about things.

He's got a mobile phone *which* can take photos.
He's got a mobile phone *that* can take photos.

When *which, that* or *who* is the object in a relative clause, we can leave it out.

We can say:
I can't find the magazine which/that I bought yesterday.
Or: *I can't find the magazine I bought yesterday.*
We can say:
There's the girl who we saw in the park yesterday.
Or: *There's the girl we saw in the park yesterday.*

6 **Make one sentence from two using *who* or *which* each time. If it is possible to leave out *who* or *which*, write them in (brackets).**

Who was that boy? He came here a minute ago.
Who was that boy who came here a minute ago?

Can you wash up the cup? You've just used it.
Can you wash up the cup (which) you've just used.

1 Did you know that old lady? We helped her in the supermarket.

....
....

2 I've broken the glass. It was on the kitchen table.

....
....

3 Let's look at the magazines. I bought them today.

....
....

4 I didn't see the man. He took Mark's wallet at the bus stop.

....
....

5 Can I have the CDs? I lent them to you on Saturday.

....
....

6 I like that singer. He was talking on the radio today.

....
....

7 **Put brackets ( ) around *that, which* or *who* if they can be left out.**

Did you like that boy (who) we met at the club?
I saw the people who live next door to you.
Have you tried the nuts (that) we bought?
I like books that make me laugh.

1 We're listening to the CD which Dave left here.
2 Can I borrow the shirt that you bought yesterday?
3 Who was that girl who you phoned a minute ago?
4 She's somebody who goes to my karate class.
5 The cinema that opened last week is very expensive.
6 The photo that you're looking at is ten years old.
7 The actor who played Romeo was amazing.
8 Here are some books which will teach you French.

8 **Put the verbs in the Present simple passive.**

These trainers ...*are made*.. (make) in the Philippines.

1 German .... (not teach) at our school.

2 I .... (expect) to help with the washing up.

3 You .... (not allow) to use your mobile phone at school.

4 The glasses ....(keep) in the middle cupboard.

5 This shampoo .... (not test) on animals.

6 The cows .... (not leave) in the field at night.

7 I .... (allow) to stay out until eleven on Saturdays.

8 Your cousin .... (invite) to Patrick's party.

9 Complete the sentences with the correct verb in the Present simple passive.

translate	give	read	play
make	~~sell~~	keep	

Stamps ...**are sold**... in supermarkets in Britain.

1 Football ……….................……. all over the world.

2 The Harry Potter books ………........……..……. into many languages.

3 This newspaper ……….........……..… by four million people every day.

4 Cheese……….......…......……. from milk.

5 We ……….......…......……. homework every day.

6 Animals in zoos ……….......…......……. in cages.

10 Match the question prompts to the answers. Then write questions with *Where, When,* or *What* and answers in the Present simple passive.

baseball (play)?   [.d.]
1 kangaroos (find)?   […]
2 the computers (keep)?   […]
3 Porsche cars (make)?   […]
4 lunch (serve)?   […]
5 your kittens (call)?   […]
6 baby sheep (call)   […]

a) at one o'clock   e) lambs
b) Fifi and Toto   f) in Australia
c) in Germany   g) in Room 28
d) ~~in the USA~~

Q: Where is baseball played?
A: It's played in the USA
1 Q: ……….......…......…….
    A: ……….......…......…….
2 Q: ……….......…......…….
    A: ……….......…......…….
3 Q: ……….......…......…….
    A: ……….......…......…….
4 Q: ……….......…......…….
    A: ……….......…......…….
5 Q: ……….......…......…….
    A: ……….......…......…….
6 Q: ……….......…......…….
    A: ……….......…......…….

11 Complete the factfile. Then rewrite the sentences in the passive leaving out the words in brackets.

The best of my country

(They) show all the latest films at the
..Astoria Cinema............... *Name a cinema.*

1 (You) eat the best food in ….................... *Name an area of your country.*

2 (They) make the best cheese in …............. …............... *Name an area of your country.*

3 (They) play the best music on …................ …............................ *Name a radio station.*

4 (They) serve the biggest ice creams at …... ….. *Name a café.*

5 (They) sell the coolest clothes at ….. *Name a shop.*

6 (They) show the funniest programmes on …............................... *Name a TV channel.*

All the latest films are shown at the......
Astoria Cinema.

1 ……….......…......…….
……….......…......…….

2 ……….......…......…….
……….......…......…….

3 ……….......…......…….
……….......…......…….

4 ……….......…......…….
……….......…......…….

5 ……….......…......…….
……….......…......…….

6 ……….......…......…….
……….......…......…….

Skills development

My favourite holiday

Read

1 The articles in a travel magazine are mixed up. Read the paragraphs marked 1 and A. Which two countries are the articles about?

1 ....

A ....

2 Read the rest of the two articles. Separate them and put the paragraphs in order by numbering them 1–5 and A–E.

[A] Last year our whole family went on holiday to Brazil for two weeks. We spent our first week in a hotel at Copacabana Beach.

[ ] On our last night we stopped in a village where there was a ceilidh (that's pronounced kay-lee.) Some musicians were playing Irish music. We all joined in and learnt some traditional Irish songs.

[...] We spent our time on the beach relaxing and watching other people. Lots of Brazilians are into gymnastics and working out. And quite a few people practise a kind of martial art called *capoeira*.

[1] We had an amazing week in Ireland last summer. We flew to Cork and hired a traditional caravan with a horse to pull it!

[...] When I wasn't watching people on the beach, I was trying the local snacks. My favourite was cold coconut milk. It's served in a coconut with a straw. I also liked the fresh prawns that are grilled on the beach and served with lime juice. Mmmm… perfect for lunch after a long swim.

[...] At night Caramel slept in fields and we slept in the caravan. It had everything we needed. There were beds, a cooker, a fridge and maps that we used all the time. Unfortunately, Caramel sometimes didn't want to follow the route that we chose.

[...] The horse was called Caramel and we soon made friends with her. We travelled around very slowly. When there was a steep hill, we had to get out and walk.

[...] It was definitely the best holiday we've ever had. But two weeks wasn't enough for that enormous country. One day I'll go back and stay longer and maybe learn to speak Portuguese.

[...] In our second week we flew from Rio de Janeiro to Salvador. It's an old town full of beautiful churches. From there we went on an expedition to Chapada Diamantina National Park where there are underground caves and swimming pools. You're given a mask and snorkel, and an underwater torch. Then you go swimming hundreds of metres underground.

[...] The next day we flew back to London. I will never forget that wonderful week when I learnt about travelling the old-fashioned way – with a horse!

3 Match the captions to the photos.

1 [...]

2 [...]

3 [...]

4 [...]

a) *Capoeira* is a kind of martial art.

b) We had a horse to pull our traditional gypsy caravan.

c) Cold coconut milk is delicious.

d) We loved the traditional Irish music.

4 Find words for the following in the text.

1 an Irish party ....

2 you wear it to see underwater ....

3 you get air through it when you're underwater

....

4 a type of seafood ....

5 a tropical drink ....

6 you drink through it ....

Write

5 **Write a travel article about one of your best holidays. Include some of these points.**

> • Where did you go? • Who with? • How long for? • Where did you stay? • What was the hotel/house like? • What did you do every day? What was the food like? • What was the weather like? • Did you travel around or go on expeditions? • Why was the holiday really good?

Begin the article like this:

The best holiday I ever had was...
....
....
....
....
....
....
....

Study tips

6 **When you don't understand a word, don't stop reading or listening. The meaning often comes after the word. Guess the meaning of these words. Write the translation next to them.**

1 There wasn't any **soap** (.....................) in the bathroom, so I couldn't wash my hands.

2 Can I have the **scissors** (.....................)? I want to cut my hair.

3 I can't stop **yawning** (.....................) . I'm really sleepy.

4 The **brakes** (.....................) on my bike didn't work so I couldn't stop.

Talk time

1 **Write the correct sentences in the speech balloons.**

- How did it go?
- Let's get started.
- I've brought a friend along.
- I didn't want to jump at first,
- Nice to meet you.
- Nice to meet you, too.

....................................,
but I really enjoyed it.

2 **Complete the dialogue with the phrases.**

- I'm afraid
- I'm afraid not
- By the way
- Hang on
- Maybe
- ~~What sort of~~

Customer I'm looking for a present for my little sister. I'd like to buy her a soft toy.

Assistant What sort of.. soft toy?

Customer I don't want to get her a teddy bear. She's already got twenty-six teddy bears. **(1)** .... a dolphin.

Assistant **(2)** .... I haven't got any dolphins.

Customer What about a giraffe or a hippopotamus?

Assistant **(3)** ....

Customer Have you got a parrot?

Assistant Yes. **(4)** .... a minute and I'll go and get you one.

Customer Wow! It's enormous. I really like it. Yes, I'll take the parrot, please.

Assistant OK, I'll put it in a bag for you. **(5)** ....,
if it won't stop talking, just take the batteries out.

Let's check

Vocabulary check

Match the words to the clues.

blinds	fridge	sink
cushions	microwave	taps
dishwasher	music system	washing machine
freezer	~~oven~~	

You make cakes in it. .oven...........................

1 You keep cold drinks in it. ....

2 You keep ice cream in it. ....

3 It washes your clothes. ....

4 It washes your dishes. ....

5 You have them over windows. ....

6 Water comes out of them. ....

7 It cooks food very fast...............................

8 You can wash dishes or vegetables in it. ....

9 You put them on chairs or sofas. ....

10 You use it to play CDs. ....

Grammar check

2 **Correct the mistakes in each sentence.**
/\ = there's a word missing; X = change one word; ⤷ = change the order of two words; * = you must delete one word.

What they are called? ⤷
What are they called?
....

1 Where is these jeans made? **X**

....

2 Let's go to a café we can have milkshakes. **/**

....
....

3 Do you know the people who they own that boat? *****

....
....

4 I really like that girl lives in the flat next door. **/**

....
....

3 **Circle the correct words for each sentence.**

The rubbish ... once a week.
A collected   **B** is collected   **C** are collected

1 All the marks ... in the teacher's notebook.
A wrote   **B** writing   **C** are written

2 She likes the purse ... you bought her in Florence.
A when   **B** whose   **C** which

3 Where is the computer ...?
A keeping   **B** keep   **C** kept

4 You ... allowed to eat sweets in class.
A not   **B** aren't   **C** don't

5 There's the boy ... the guitar at the club.
A which played   **B** played   **C** who played

6 I've got a friend ... father is a pilot.
A that   **B** whose   **C** which

7 We're going to the hotel ... we stayed last year.
A which   **B** that   **C** where

8 ... expected to tidy my room once a week.
A I'm   **B** It   **C** I'll

9 Did you know the boy ... spoke to in the park?
A which we   **B** what we   **C** we

10 Can I have the books ... gave you last week?
A what I   **B** I   **C** when I

4 **Make sentences by putting the words in order.**

Breakfast / from / is / nine / served / seven / until
Breakfast is served from seven until nine.

1 are / do / expected / to / What / we / ?

....

2 all / CDs / He's / him / I / lent / lost / the / which

....
....

3 a beach / can / go / Let's / to / we / where / surf

....
....

GRAMMAR FILE

Pronouns:

somebody, anybody, nobody, everybody

There's somebody on the phone for you.

I know somebody who lives in that building.

Does anybody want a piece of cake?

We didn't know anybody at the party.

Nobody told me about the test.

Everybody had a great time at the picnic.

Pronouns:

something, anything, nothing, everything

There's something wrong with my bike.

I've got something in my eye.

Would you like anything from the shops?

She didn't eat anything for breakfast.

There's nothing to eat in the fridge.

I'll tell you everything in a minute.

Pronouns:

somewhere, anywhere, nowhere, everywhere

Let's go somewhere quiet to talk.

I can't see my jacket anywhere.

We didn't go anywhere. We just stayed at home.

There's nowhere to sit. Let's go somewhere else for a coffee.

We looked for you everywhere. Where were you?

- We can also use *-one* instead of *-body*: *someone, anyone, no one, everyone*, e.g. *I met someone really interesting yesterday. Do you know anyone who has a horse? No one knows Judy's new phone number. Everyone was singing and dancing on New Year's Eve.*

- We usually use *somebody, someone, something* and *somewhere* in affirmative statements, e.g. *There's someone in the bathroom. I've got something for you. They're going somewhere special for dinner.* We also use them in questions when we offer things, e.g. *Would you like something to eat?*

- We usually use *anybody, anyone, anything* and *anywhere* in questions and negative statements, e.g. *Is anybody at home? I haven't got anything to wear to the party. Don't go anywhere until I get back.*

- We also use *anybody, anyone, anything* and *anywhere* when we mean 'I don't mind who …/what…/where…', e.g. *'What would you like to do tomorrow?" 'Anything. You decide.' 'Where would you like to go?' 'Anywhere. It doesn't matter.'*

- With *nobody, no one, nothing* and *nowhere*, we don't use a negative verb, e.g. *He ate nothing.* (= He didn't eat anything.) *They went nowhere.* (= They didn't go anywhere.)

- The *some-, any-, no-, every-* pronouns all take a singular verb, e.g. *Everyone likes holidays. No one wants to get up early tomorrow.* But we use *their, they* and *them* after these pronouns, e.g. *Has everyone got their tickets? Did anyone leave their purse here yesterday? If anyone phones, tell them to call again later.*

Reported commands

Affirmative

Command	Reported command
'Go away, Joey.'	He told Joey to go away.
'Please leave.'	She asked me to leave.
'Call me later, Rob.'	He told Rob to call him later.

Negative

Command	Reported command
'Please don't tell anyone.'	He asked me not to tell anyone.
'Don't make a noise, Tom.'	She told Tom not to make a noise.
'Please don't laugh, Amy.'	She asked Amy not to laugh.

- Commands are in the imperative, e.g. *Go away! Please come back. Don't write on the desks.*
- When we report commands, we use the verbs *tell* or *ask* + an object + the infinitive with *to*, e.g. *He told me to go away. She asked me to come back. The teacher told us not to write on the desk.*
- To report negative commands, we use the verbs *tell* or *ask* + an object + *not* + the infinitive with *to*, e.g. *She asked me not to tell anyone. I told him not to talk about it.*

Second conditional: *if* + Past simple .... *'d/would/wouldn't*

If I had her phone number, I'd call her now.
If you won £1,000, what would you do with the money?
She'd be really angry with you if she knew.
I wouldn't lend him your bike if I were you.

- We use the second conditional to talk about a situation which is unlikely to happen, e.g. *If you had a lot of money, what would you do with it?* We also use it to talk about situations which are a complete fantasy, e.g. *If I met David Beckham I'd ask him to play football with me.* We can also use it to give advice, e.g. *If I were you, I'd ask your parents first.*
- Second conditional sentences are formed with *if* + the Past simple tense and *would* + the base form of the verb in the main clause, e.g. *If I had a horse, I would go riding on the beach every day.*
- The *if*-clause can come before or after the main clause. When the *if*-clause comes first, it is separated from the main clause by a comma, e.g. *If I knew the answer, I'd tell you.* BUT: *I'd tell you if I knew the answer.*
- The phrase *If I were you ...* is more common than *If I was you ... .*

Somebody's always late

Vocabulary

1 It's a bad day at the sports club. Eleven people have got problems. Read the sentences then write the correct name under each picture.

- Andy's arm is bleeding.
- Ben has broken his arm.
- Fran has got a cold.
- Sue has got a temperature.
- Liam has got toothache.
- ~~Sam has got a sore throat.~~
- Serena's got a headache.
- Dan has got a pain in his stomach.
- Erica feels dizzy.
- Rob has hurt his knee.
- Hannah has sprained her wrist.

.......Sam.......   1 ....

2 ....   3 ....

4 ....   5 ....

6 ....   7 ....   8 ....   9 ....   10 ....

Dialogue work

2 Complete the dialogue with the correct word.

brown	call	competition	dishwasher	horse	thousand	what	~~won~~	farm	games

Adam What would you do if you won lots of money?

Dominic You mean in a (**1**)..................................... ?

Adam Yes. What would you do if you won a (**2**)......................... pounds for example?

Dominic I'd buy a (**3**)................................. for Mum. I'd never have to do the washing up again.

Adam But (**4**)............... would you get for yourself?

Dominic I'd buy a (**5**).................., I think. I could keep it on Eddie's (**6**)..........................., maybe.

Adam Cool. Then we could all go round to Eddie's and ride it. What would you (**7**)............... it?

Dominic If it was a white horse, I'd call it Starlight. If it was (**8**)....................., I'd call it Choco. What would you do?

Adam I'd probably buy a season ticket for Arsenal. Then I could go and watch all their (**9**).......................

Grammar practice

3 **Choose the correct word in each sentence.**

(Anybody / (Somebody)) has eaten all my chocolates.

1 We were too far from the stage. We didn't see (nothing / anything).

2 He isn't happy at the moment. He's worried about (everything / anything).

3 Hello? Is (everybody / anybody) there? Hello?

4 I don't know (anybody / somebody) who likes getting up early.

5 I hate this place. There are spiders (everywhere / anywhere).

6 Just stay here for a minute. Don't go (anywhere / nowhere).

7 (Somebody / Everybody) really enjoyed the picnic.

8 (Someone / No one) gave me two tickets to the concert. Do you want to come with me?

9 (Something / Anything) strange is happening. What is going on?

10 There's (nothing / something) you can do to help. So just sit down and relax.

11 We stayed here last weekend. We didn't go (somewhere / anywhere).

12 (Anyone / No one) in my family has ever seen a ghost.

4 **Complete the sentences with pronouns beginning *some-* , *any-*, *every-* or *no-*.**

'What do you want to do tomorrow?' '.Anything.. I don't mind. You choose.'

1 I didn't buy .... at the airport shops. .... was too expensive for me.

2 I don't want .... to eat, thanks. I feel sick.

3 I heard a voice. I think there's .... in the garden.

4 OK, ... , this is important so please listen.

5 There's .... in this envelope. I think it's a CD.

6 This village is boring. There's .... to do and .... to go.

7 What's the matter? I know you're upset about ....

5 **Complete the sentences truthfully.**

Almost everybody likes ..chocolate..... .

1 Almost everybody likes ....
....

2 Nobody in my family ....
....

3 I don't know anybody who ....
....

4 I know somebody who ....
....

5 Next summer I'd like to go somewhere ....
....

6 **Match the people to what they said. Then report their requests using *told* or *asked*.**

[c.] The doctor told me to open my mouth and say, 'Aaah'.

[e.] My little sister asked me to help her with her Maths.

1 [...] The dentist ....
....

2 [...] My pen-friend ....
....

3 [...] The photographer ....
....

4 [...] The football coach ....
....

5 [...] My teacher ....
....

6 [...] My mother ....
....

a) Please take Truffles for a walk.

b) Clean your teeth after every meal.

c) ~~Open your mouth and say, 'Aaah'.~~

d) Do Exercise 3 again.

e) ~~Please help me with my Maths.~~

f) Look at the camera and smile.

g) Stay near the goal.

h) Please send a photo of your family.

8

7 **Match the sentence beginnings in A with the commands in B. Then complete each sentence with the correct reported command.**

A

[f.] Mum and Dad were asleep so I told ..Jack.....
   ..not.to.play.the.guitar...

1 [...] It was a dangerous road so I told ....
   ....

2 [...] It was a secret so I told ....
   ....

3 [...] My camera was broken so I asked ....
   ....

4 [...] I was really hungry so I asked ....
   ....

5 [...] I was in a bad mood so I told ....
   ....

6 [...] I felt dizzy so I asked ....
   ....

B

a) Ben, don't ask me silly questions.
b) Chloe, don't eat my chips.
c) Dad, can you repair it?
d) Eleanor, don't drive too fast.
e) Fran, can you get me a glass of water?
f) Jack, don't play the guitar.
g) Seth, don't tell anyone.

8 **Match the sentence halves and write the complete sentence.**

[c.] If he had enough money,
   ..he'd buy a new guitar..........................

1 [...] If she ate more fruit and vegetables, ...
   ....

2 [...] The town would be cleaner ....
   ....

3 [...] If you had a computer,................................
   ....

4 [...] If I were you, ...
   ....

5 [...] It would be great ....

6 [...] She wouldn't like it ....
   ....

a) I wouldn't listen to Alice.   **e)** if there weren't any cars.
b) if I won this competition.   **f)** if you read her diary.
c) he'd buy a new guitar.   **g)** you could send me
d) she'd be healthier.   e-mails.

9 **Write sentences in the second conditional using the verbs in brackets.**

If I ..had. (have) lots of money, I ..would.buy.. (buy) a new skateboard.

1 He...(look) better if he sometimes .... (comb) his hair.

2 We ....(not have) to do the washing up if we ....(have) a dishwasher.

3 What .... (you like) to be if you ....(can) choose any job in the world?

4 I .... (not go) and see that film if I ....(be) you.

5 If I ....(know) Patrick's number, I .... (call) him now.

6 If you ....(have) one wish, what .... (you ask) for?

10 **Complete the second conditional sentences.**

If I met ..David.Beckham,.I'd.ask.him.to.play....
   ..football.with.me,.. .

1 If I could have any job, I'd be ....
   ....

2 If I had a lot of money, ...
   ....

3 If I could go anywhere in the world, ...
   ....

4 If I had ...., ...
   ....

5 If I was ...., ...
   ....

11 Complete the quiz questions. Then choose an answer and write it with *I'd* …

THE TEMPO HORROR QUIZ
Are you a cool cat or a nervous mouse?
Find out with this quiz!

What would you do if you ..couldn't.... (can't) find the way out of a dark forest?

- [ ] a) cry
- [ ] b) wait for someone to come and find me
- [✓] c) phone my mum on my mobile

I'd phone my mum on my mobile.

1 What would you do if there ……………(be) a ghost in your bedroom?

- [ ] a) cry
- [ ] b) hide under the bed
- [ ] c) tell it to go away

………………………………………………………

2 What would you do if a bull ……………(run) towards you in a field?

- [ ] a) run away
- [ ] b) sit down on the grass
- [ ] c) jump on it and ride it

………………………………………………………

3 What would you do if you ………… (cut) your finger badly?

- a) cry
- b) call an ambulance
- c) show it to my parents

………………………………………………………

Score 1 point for a) answers.
Score 2 points for b) answers.
Score 3 points for c) answers.

4 What would you do if you ……………(find) a big spider in your shoe?

- [ ] a) call the police
- [ ] b) call the zoo
- [ ] c) take a photo of it

………………………………………………………

5 What would you do if you ………………………(drop) your father's expensive camera on the floor?

- [ ] a) say nothing
- [ ] b) say sorry
- [ ] c) start saving my pocket money

………………………………………………………

6 What would you do if you ……………(wake) up and you …………………(can't) remember your name?

- [ ] a) stay in bed for the day
- [ ] b) ask a friend about my name
- [ ] c) choose a nice new name

………………………………………………………

Analysis

15–18:

Cool cat! You can always see a way out of every difficult situation. People think you are a very exciting person.

10–14:

You're Mr or Miss Sensible. You're a kind person and you understand people's problems. But your life would be more fun if you had a bit more courage.

6–9:

Nervous mouse! You're frightened of everything. Be careful of this book. It might fall off the table and hurt your foot!

Boo!

Culture spot

Cornwall

Cornwall, in the extreme southwest of Britain, is famous for its small fishing villages, its spectacular coast and its beautiful sandy beaches. It's got the sunniest weather in Britain, the cleanest sea and the best surfing. So it's not surprising that it's a very popular holiday spot.

Tourism hasn't always been big in Cornwall. With the Atlantic Ocean on three sides, and the Tamar river as its **border** on the fourth side, Cornwall is almost an island. A hundred and fifty years ago nobody visited the place. It even had its own language until the eighteenth century. It was a Celtic language because the Cornish people, like the Scots, the Irish and the Welsh, are related to the Celts, a group of people who arrived in Britain around 1000 BC.

WALES   ENGLAND

Cornwall

There are a lot of rocks along the coast of Cornwall. These are dangerous for ships and have caused a lot of **shipwrecks**. In the eighteenth century, 'wrecking' was a way of life for many Cornish people. Sometimes hundreds of people followed a ship along the coast. If it got into difficulties, they would wait for it to crash on the rocks, then **steal** its **cargo**. **Smuggling** was also common at this time. The Cornish coast was full of **tunnels** and caves where **smugglers** used to hide **brandy**, tea and tobacco because they didn't want to pay tax on them.

Cornwall used to make its money from metals like **tin** and **copper**. But the tin and copper **mines** are closed now. Fishing is still important, but Cornwall's biggest industry is tourism.

1 Read the text and write T (true) or F (false).

1 You can go surfing in Cornwall. ....

2 Not many people visit Cornwall. ....

3 People in Cornwall don't speak English. ....

4 Parts of the Cornish coast are dangerous for boats. ....

5 There isn't a fishing industry in Cornwall any more. ....

2 Match the meanings to the words.

1 [h] border   **7** [...] smugglers

2 [...] shipwrecks   **8** [...] brandy

3 [...] steal   **9** [...] tin

4 [...] cargo   **10** [...] copper

5 [...] smuggling   **11** [...] mines

6 [...] tunnels

a) an alcoholic drink

b) bringing something into the country without paying tax

c) a soft metal, sometimes used for roofs (Sn in chemistry)

d) paths under the ground

e) criminals who bring things into the country without paying tax

f) a red-brown metal (Cu in chemistry)

g) take something from another person

h) ~~the line between two countries or states~~

i) the things a boat is carrying

j) very deep holes in the ground where people take out metal

k) when ships are broken on rocks or in a storm

3 Read about some places to visit in Cornwall. Match four of the places to the photos. Write the numbers in the boxes next to the photos.

Places to visit in Cornwall

1 **The Minack**
This open-air theatre has an amazing view of the sea.

2 **Tintagel**
The ruins of a castle and a spectacular view make this a magic place.

3 **The Seal Sanctuary**
Here they take care of young seals who have lost their parents in storms at sea.

4 **The Tate Gallery, St Ives**
If you love art, this is the place for you.

5 **Mousehole**
This is possibly the prettiest fishing village in Cornwall.

6 **Porthcurno Beach**
There are 15 kilometres of golden sand and turquoise blue water. Don't try and surf here unless you're an expert.

7 **The Eden Project**
It has the largest greenhouse in the world. It's 50 metres high and contains a rainforest!

Portfolio

4 Write about a tourist area or town in your country. List five interesting places to visit and write a sentence about each one. Use the *Places to visit in Cornwall* as a model.

Places to visit in ....
....
....
....
....
....
....
....
....
....
....
....
....
....
....
....
....

a [...]

c [...]

b [...]

d [...]

Let's read

A good day out

1 Write the missing parts of the dialogue in the correct gaps.

- And you don't need to bring your own fishing lines.
- That's in about ten minutes.
- We need to buy some sun cream first.
- We'd like to go on the fishing trip.
- We've only got two places left.
- What time does the boat leave?
- ~~Which boat trip were you thinking of?~~

Anna:	Is this the right place to buy tickets for a boat trip?		....	
Boatman:	Yes, it is. .Which boat trip were you. .thinking of?..........................	**Anna:**	How much is it?	
		Boatman:	That'll be £7 each please.	
	We've got two this morning – a fishing trip and a birdwatching trip.	**Anna:**	Here you are.	
		Boatman:	Thank you.	
Anna:	(1)	**Anna:**	(4)	
Boatman:	That's on this boat.	**Boatman:**	At eleven fifteen. (5)	
Anna:	The Bluebird?		But you can get on the boat now if you like.	
Boatman:	Yes, that's right. It's a three hour trip. (2)	**Anna:**	(6)	
	We give you them. How many of you are there?	**Boatman:**	Very sensible. You can get some at the shop at the end of the pier.	
Anna:	Just me and my friend.			
Boatman:	That's good. (3)			

2 Use the dialogue to complete the information board.

A .....fishing.........TRIP

NAME OF BOAT: ....

THE TRIP LASTS: ....

WE GIVE YOU: ....

PRICE PER PERSON: ....

BOAT LEAVES AT: ....

Let's check

Vocabulary check

1 **Choose the correct word for each sentence.**

bleeding	hurt	sick
~~broken~~	pain	sore

Sue came back from her skiing holiday with a ..broken..... wrist. Now she can't ride her bike for six weeks.

1 Actors and singers often get .... throats because they use their voice a lot.

2 Dan's got a .... in his stomach. I think he's eaten something bad.

3 I always feel .... when I travel by coach.

4 Lily's hand is .... She did it with a knife when she was cutting up onions.

5 My legs .... today because we went on a three-hour walk yesterday.

Grammar check

2 **Correct the mistake in each sentence.**
/\ = there's a word missing; X = change one word; ↪ = change the order of two words; * = you must delete one word.

I didn't meet nobody nice at the party. **X**
I didn't meet anybody nice at the party.

1 If I were you, I wouldn't to eat that cake. *****

....
....

2 Milly asked me wait for her. **/**

....

3 I think Orlando is anywhere in the United States. **X**

....
....

4 Mum told us not stay up late. **/**

....

5 Which videos you would buy if you had the money? **↪**

....
....

3 **Circle the correct words for each sentence.**

... in my class likes sending e-mails and messages. We all do it in our lunch breaks.
A Nobody **B** Somebody **C** Everybody ⟵circled

1 There's ... in my class who can move their ears up and down.
A somebody **B** anybody **C** everybody

2 My parents always tell me ... a cycle helmet.
A wearing **B** to wear **C** to wearing

3 Football is his life. ... is more important to him.
A Something **B** Anything **C** Nothing

4 I told you ... in the bag under my bed.
A not look **B** not looking **C** not to look

5 Let's go somewhere else. ... in this shop is too expensive.
A Something **B** Anything **C** Everything

6 If I ... £1,000, I would buy lots of new clothes.
A win **B** will win **C** won

7 I'm not going ... today. I'm cold and tired and I want to stay at home.
A nowhere **B** anywhere **C** everywhere

8 Don't say ... about the party to Freddie. I haven't invited him.
A nothing **B** everything **C** anything

9 What ... say to Britney Spears if you met her in the street?
A would you **B** will you **C** did you

10 Please get a plate. You are dropping bits of cake ...
A everywhere **B** anywhere **C** somewhere

1 **Match the signs (A–H) to the meanings (1–5). There are two extra signs.**

EXAMPLE

0 This dog sometimes bites   [B]

1 When you buy two of these, you only
pay for one.   [...]

2 Don't waste electricity.   [...]

3 Put sweet papers, chewing gum, etc in the bin. [...]

4 You can walk by the sea here.   [...]

5 It's cheaper to buy three of these.   [...]

A BUY ONE GET ONE FREE

B DANGEROUS DOG

C ★ SAVE ENERGY ★

D DON'T DROP LITTER

E STAY SAFE IN THE SUN

F NOW RECYCLE THIS

G COASTAL PATH

H PENS £1 EACH OR 3 FOR £2.50

2 **Complete the article about teddy bears with the correct words. Circle A, B or C for each space.**

You probably know **0** teddy bears are the world's most popular toys. But you might not know that they are also **1** most collectable toys. Collectors buy **2** sell teddy bears all over the world. Unusual teddy bears **3** be very valuable. The **4** price that anyone has paid so far is £130,000. That **5** in 2000 for a bear **6** Teddy Girl.

Are you feeling upset now because you **7** thrown away all your old teddy bears? Well, **8** worry too much! Most teddy bears **9** not valuable. To be valuable, teddy bears **10** to be more than forty years old. There's **11** point buying new bears. You will have **12** a very long time before they are valuable. It **13** better if you asked your grandmother about her teddy bears. She might **14** a valuable one **15** in her house!

EXAMPLE

0	**A** because	**B** that	**C** a
1	**A** some	**B** for	**C** the
2	**A** for	**B** and	**C** so
3	**A** can	**B** are	**C** always
4	**A** higher	**B** high	**C** highest
5	**A** is	**B** was	**C** will be
6	**A** call	**B** name's	**C** called
7	**A** have	**B** did	**C** were
8	**A** no	**B** must	**C** don't
9	**A** was	**B** will	**C** are
10	**A** must	**B** have	**C** will
11	**A** any	**B** nothing	**C** no
12	**A** waiting	**B** wait	**C** to wait
13	**A** will be	**B** would be	**C** was
14	**A** have	**B** had	**C** having
15	**A** nowhere	**B** somewhere	**C** everywhere

3 Read the article about tea. Are sentences 1–10 'Right' (A) or 'Wrong' (B)? If there isn't enough information to answer 'Right' or 'Wrong', choose 'Doesn't say' (C).

A nice cup of tea!

Tea is a very important drink in Britain. At least 77% of British people drink three or four cups of tea a day. More than 185 million cups of tea are drunk every day in Britain. A lot of British people drink tea first with breakfast, then at eleven o'clock, then with lunch, then at four o'clock, then at dinner time, and finally just before bed. Only 23% of British people drink coffee more often than tea.

Most people use tea bags to make tea, but some serious tea-drinkers still make tea in the traditional way. First the water is boiled. Then some of the boiling water is used to make the teapot warm. Then the tea leaves are put in the teapot. Then the boiling water is added. Then the pot is left for five minutes under a 'tea cosy'. A tea cosy is a sort of jacket that keeps the teapot warm. Finally, the tea is served in delicate cups with saucers.

The word 'tea' is used in a lot of different ways in the English language. A lot of people call their dinner their tea, even if they don't drink tea with it. If someone is upset, they need 'tea and sympathy'. And there's the expression 'a storm in a teacup'. It means that people are making trouble about something that isn't important.

EXAMPLE

0 Most British people drink tea every day.
   A Right (circled)
   B Wrong
   C Doesn't say

1 British people never drink tea after dinner.
   A Right   **B** Wrong   **C** Doesn't say

2 British people make bad coffee.
   A Right   **B** Wrong   **C** Doesn't say

3 Tea made with tea bags is not very good.
   A Right   **B** Wrong   **C** Doesn't say

4 These days nobody makes tea in a teapot.
   A Right   **B** Wrong   **C** Doesn't say

5 Most people in Britain drink tea with milk and sugar.
   A Right   **B** Wrong   **C** Doesn't say

6 A tea cosy helps to keep the teapot warm.
   A Right   **B** Wrong   **C** Doesn't say

7 Some people call dinner, tea.
   A Right   **B** Wrong   **C** Doesn't say

8 'A storm in a teacup' means the weather is very bad.
   A Right   **B** Wrong   **C** Doesn't say

9 Drinking tea is good for your health.
   A Right   **B** Wrong   **C** Doesn't say

4 Complete the article about superstition with the correct words. Circle A, B or C for each space.

Superstition

0 you believe in luck? Have you **1** a lucky number? Or a lucky colour? If you answer yes to one **2** those questions, then you are probably superstitious. **3** worry about it. Around 76% of people in Britain admit that they are **4** bit superstitious.

Superstitions exist in **5** country but they aren't always **6** same. For example, in Britain people **7** wood for luck. But in Italy it's lucky **8** touch iron. In Britain, the number thirteen is **9** unlucky. **10** there an unlucky number in your country?

EXAMPLE

0 A Are   **B Do** (circled)   **C** Does

1 **A** choose   **B** your   **C** got
2 **A** of   **B** for   **C** from
3 **A** Mustn't   **B** Don't   **C** Stop
4 **A** some   **B** a   **C** little
5 **A** all   **B** most   **C** every
6 **A** the   **B** for   **C** your
7 **A** touching   **B** touched.   **C** touch
8 **A** for   **B** to   **C** if
9 **A** too   **B** the   **C** very
10 **A** Is   **B** Was   **C** Has

GRAMMAR FILE

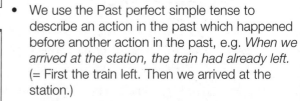

Past perfect simple

Affirmative

Long form	Short form
I had started.	I'd started.
You had started.	You'd started.
She had started.	She'd started.
He had started.	He'd started.
It had started.	_____
We had started.	We'd started.
You had started.	You'd started.
They had started.	They'd started.

Negative

Long form	Short form
I had not started.	I hadn't started.
You had not started.	You hadn't started.
She had not started.	She hadn't started.
He had not started.	He hadn't started.
It had not started.	It hadn't started.
We had not started.	We hadn't started.
You had not started.	You hadn't started.
They had not started.	They hadn't started.

Questions

Had I started?
Had you started?
Had she started?
Had he started?
Had it started?
Had we started?
Had you started?
Had they started?

Short answers

Affirmative	Negative
Yes, I had.	No, I hadn't.
Yes, you had.	No, you hadn't.
Yes, she had.	No, she hadn't.
Yes, he had.	No, he hadn't.
Yes, it had.	No, it hadn't.
Yes, we had.	No, we hadn't.
Yes, you had.	No, you hadn't.
Yes, they had.	No, they hadn't.

Wh? questions

What had I / you / we/ they started?
What had she / he / it started?

- We use the Past perfect simple tense to describe an action in the past which happened before another action in the past, e.g. *When we arrived at the station, the train had already left.* (= First the train left. Then we arrived at the station.)
- We form the Past perfect simple with *had* and the past participle, e.g. *had started, had done, had arrived.*
- The Past perfect of the verb *have* is *had had*, e.g. *She didn't eat lunch because she had had a very big breakfast.*
- With some irregular verbs, the past participle is different from the Past simple. There is a list of irregular verbs on page 135 of the Student's Book.
- The verb *go* has two past participles: *been* and *gone.*
- We use *gone* to say that someone had gone away and hadn't yet returned, e.g. *Lucy wasn't at the party because she had gone to Ireland.* (= She was in still in Ireland.)
- We use *been* to say that someone had been away and had returned, e.g. *Rob looked really relaxed. He had been in Cornwall for a week.* (= He went to Cornwall for a week then he came back.)

Reported statements

Direct speech

Maria: 'I'm going swimming.'

Andy: 'I don't want to go just yet.'

Maria: 'I'm leaving in five minutes.'

Andy: 'I cycled to the beach on Saturday.'

Maria: 'I've made sandwiches for lunch.'

Andy: 'I'll come after lunch.'

Maria: 'We can meet at the Beach Café.'

Reported speech

Maria said that she was going swimming.

Andy said that he that didn't want to go just yet.

Maria said that she was leaving in five minutes.

Andy said that he had cycled to the beach on Saturday.

Maria said that she had made sandwiches for lunch.

Andy said that he would come after lunch.

Maria said that they could meet at the Beach Café.

- When we report statements, we use the verbs *say* or *tell* and (if we want) the word *that*, e.g. *She said that she was very tired. She said she was very tired. She told me that she was very tired. She told me she was very tired.*

- There are rules for tense changes after past reporting verbs like *said* and *told*.

Direct speech	Reported speech
Present simple	Past simple
Present continuous	Past continuous
Past simple	Past perfect
Present perfect	Past perfect
am/are/is	*was/were*
have/has	*had*
do/does	*did*
can/will	*could/would*

- There are no tense changes if the reporting verb is in the present tense, e.g. Lily: 'I don't want to come.' *Lily says she doesn't want to come.* Nick: 'I'm going swimming later.' *Nick says that he's going swimming later.*

say and *tell*

Maria said that she was going swimming.

Maria told Andy that she was going swimming

Andy said that he didn't want to go just yet.

Andy told her that he didn't want to go just yet.

Maria said that she was leaving in five minutes.

Maria told him that she was leaving in five minutes.

- The verb *tell* is followed by an object noun or pronoun, e.g. *She told Josie she didn't want to go out. Nick told us he was angry with his brother.*

- The verb *say* is not followed by an object noun or pronoun but it can be followed by *to* + object noun or pronoun, e.g. *She said to Josie that she didn't want to go out. Nick said to us that he was angry with his brother.*

Third conditional: *if* + Past perfect … , *would have/ could have* + past participle

If you'd listened to me, this wouldn't have happened.

If I'd had my camera with me, I could have taken some amazing photos.

We would have had more fun if you'd been there too.

I'd have lent you some money if you'd asked me.

- We use third conditional sentences to talk about things which might have happened, but didn't happen, e.g. *If I'd had his number, I would have called him.* (= I didn't have his number so I didn't call him.)

- We form the third conditional with *if* + Past perfect, *would have/could have* + past participle.

- The *if*-clause can come before or after the main clause. When the *if*-clause comes first, it is separated from the main clause by a comma, e.g. *If I'd had my money with me, I'd have bought those trainers.* BUT: *I'd have bought those trainers if I'd had my money with me.*

I'd gone to the cinema

Vocabulary

1 **Label the pictures with the correct words.**

bus stop	~~office block~~	tower block
cycle lane	pavement	traffic lights
crossroads	roundabout	zebra crossing
lamp post	T-junction	

office block

1 ....

2 ....

3 ....

4 ....

5 ....

6 ....

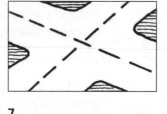

7 ....

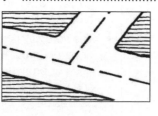

8 ....

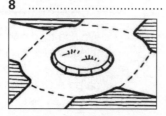

9 ....

10 ....

2 **Look at the picture and fill the gaps with the correct words.**

bridge	hedge	gate	field
fence	signpost	~~footpath~~	stream

Walk along the ..**footpath**..... . On your left there's a
(**1**)…….............…… and on your right there's a
(**2**)………….......…. At the end of the footpath there's a
(**3**)……...…..… Go through it. Don't forget to shut it,
so the moon cows can't get out of the (**4**)………….
In front of you, you will see a (**5**)……...............… with
jumping fish in it. Don't put your hands or feet in the
water. The fish are dangerous and they might hurt
you. To cross, you must go over the (**6**)……...........… .
On the other side, you will see a (**7**)………...….......…
that says TO THE SPACE STATION.

Dialogue work

3 **Complete the dialogue with the correct words.**

fun	night	oven	plates	trouble
ham	not	~~party~~	plenty	walk

Eloisa What was your dad's birthday .....party.. like?

Eddie It was (1).............. but we had a bit of trouble with the food.

Eloisa What do you mean? What kind of (2).............?

Eddie Well, in the morning Mum put lots of cold chicken and (3)............. on big plates. Then we all went out for a (4)..............

Eloisa And what happened?

Eddie When we got back, there was nothing on the (5)............. and Perkins, our cat, looked really happy.

Eloisa You're joking.

Eddie No, I'm (6)...................... Perkins had eaten everything.

Eloisa What did you do?

Eddie There was (7)............. of other food to eat.

Eloisa What about the birthday cake? You were making it last (8)............. when I phoned.

Eddie We couldn't eat it.

Eloisa Why not?

Eddie Because I'd forgotten to turn on the (9)............. so it wasn't cooked!

Grammar practice

4 **Match each sentence beginning to the correct ending. Put the verbs in brackets in the Past perfect simple.**

[f.] I borrowed some money because ....

I had spent all mine...............................

1 [...] His room was a mess because ....

....

2 [...] I didn't sleep because ....

....

3 [...] They lost the match because...........................

....

4 [...] I felt sick because...

....

5 [...] The house was dark because ....

....

6 [...] We didn't recognise her because ....

....

7 [...] He forgot his lines because ....

....

8 [...] She was upset because ....

....

a) she (have) a fight with her best friend

b) I (drink) three cups of coffee

c) she (cut) her hair

d) they (not practise) enough

e) everyone (go) out

f) ~~I (spend) all mine~~

g) I (ate) too much cake

h) he (not) learn them very well

i) he (not tidy) it for a week

5 **Fill the gaps with a verb in the Past perfect simple.**

drink	lose	not fly	throw
not play	~~rain~~	make	

The grass was wet because it **had rained.** in the night.

1 I asked Sara for the magazine but she .... it away.

2 I was scared on the plane because I .... before.

3 There wasn't any orange juice because Gaby .... it all.

4 I didn't win the tennis game because I .... for a long time.

5 They climbed through the window because they .... the keys.

6 We ate all the sandwiches that Melissa .... for us.

9

6 **Write sentences in the Past perfect simple.**

Andrea didn't want to go to a restaurant.

(She / just / eat / a sandwich)

<u>She had just eaten a sandwich.</u>

1 I saw Milly Bennett last week.

(She / not change)

....

2 We arrived at the cinema late.

(We / miss / ten minutes)

....

3 There was water everywhere.

(He / not turn off / the taps)

....

4 Amy wasn't at home.

(She / go / swimming)

....

5 My mother and I went to see *Titanic*.

(She / not see / it)

....

6 Toby was hungry.

(Nobody / give / him / dinner)

....

7 **Fill the gaps with *say/said* or *tell/told*.**

Mark ..<u>said</u>...he was hungry.

What did he .<u>tell</u>.. you?

1 Did Sylvia .... she'd be back by nine?

2 Josh .... me he had a sore throat.

3 Please don't .... Anna about the party.

4 I'll .... you a secret about my little brother.

5 Did Liza .... she was going to the concert?

6 Mrs Stanton .... she didn't like dogs.

7 Did that man .... you he was a policeman?

8 Jo asked us about the letter but we didn't .... him anything.

9 Justin asked me about Imogen but I didn't .... anything.

10 Please don't .... me another stupid joke.

8 **Report what young British actor Dinesh Kumar said in a recent interview.**

I really enjoy being an actor.

1 I meet lots of interesting people.

2 Last year I was in a film about skateboarders.

3 I had skateboarding lessons every day.

4 I can skateboard really well now.

5 I'm going to India in September to make a film.

6 I'll be there for about six months.

7 I have lots of cousins in India.

8 My parents are going to visit me.

9 I'm not looking forward to the plane journey.

10 I don't like flying very much.

<u>He said he really enjoyed being an actor.</u>

1 ....

2 ....

3 ....

4 ....

5 ....

6 ....

7 ....

8 ....

9 ....

10 ....

9 Complete the sentences with verbs in the Past perfect simple.

If I .'d had.. (have) my camera, I would have taken a photo.

1 We'd have met you at the airport if you
……………..…...……………. (call) us.

2 If you ………….....…………….. (not go) swimming in that lake, you wouldn't have got ill.

3 Mrs Dalton wouldn't have been so angry if we
……………………………… (tidy) the room.

4 Toby would have eaten your dinner if I
……………………………… (not stop) him.

5 If we ……………………………. (have) a map, we wouldn't have got lost.

6 I wouldn't have got the main part in the school play if Jody ……………………………… (not be) ill.

10 Complete the sentences in the third conditional.

The party .would have been. (be) OK if there'd been some good music.

1 If you'd phoned, we …………………………………… (not be) so worried.

2 You …………………………… (get) a better mark if you'd done more work.

3 If you'd seen her face, you ……………………………
……………………………………(not laugh).

4 I ……………………………………… (phone) you if I'd had my mobile phone with me.

5 If I'd remembered her birthday, I …………………………
…………………………(send) her a card.

6 She ………………………………………… (not cut) her hand if she'd been more careful.

7 If we'd known about the party, we …………………………
…………………………… (not go) to the cinema.

8 You …………………………………… (hurt) yourself if you'd dived in there.

11 Match the sentence halves. Then write sentences in the third conditional.

[.b.] If the music (not be) so awful
1 [...] She (be) really angry
2 [...] If you (not make) all that noise
3 [...] I (make) a cake
4 [...] If we (know) about the insects
5 [...] My mother (be) a ballet dancer
6 [...] We (laugh)

a) if he (say) anything funny
b) ~~we (stay) at the party~~
c) if she (see) that mess
d) we (not go) camping there
e) if she (not be) in a car accident
f) I (sleep) well
g) if I (have) some eggs

If the music hadn't been so awful
we would have stayed at the party.

1 ……………………………………………………
……………………………………………………
……………………………………………………

2 ……………………………………………………
……………………………………………………
……………………………………………………

3 ……………………………………………………
……………………………………………………
……………………………………………………

4 ……………………………………………………
……………………………………………………
……………………………………………………

5 ……………………………………………………
……………………………………………………
……………………………………………………

6 ……………………………………………………
……………………………………………………

Little girl with a big voice

Christina Aguilera (1)..................................
.... when she was only three. She
used to put a towel on the floor as her stage,
stand on it and sing through a stick which she
called her 'icaphone' – microphone. Now she's
one of the biggest names in pop and Christina
loves it. But life hasn't always been easy for her.

Christina Maria Aguilera was born on the 18th
December 1980 in Staten Island, New York. Her
father, Fausto Aguilera, an Ecuadorian-American,
was in the US **army**, so the family moved around
a lot. 'It was difficult for me,' says Christina,
'because we didn't stay in the same place very
long. We lived in New Jersey, Texas and Japan.
Every time we moved, (2)..............................
.... I'm still a bit jealous of people who
have had the same best friend since they were
little.' Christina's parents divorced when she was
quite young and she carried on living with her
mother. She spent her teenage years in Wexford,
Pennsylvania.

At the age of eight, she was on a TV show called
Star Search. Christina soon discovered the
disadvantages of being a **celebrity**. Christina's
mom Shelly says, 'Sometimes she missed school
(3).. Some of
the kids at her school didn't like that. They were
mean to her because she was different. In the
end we moved house.'

At twelve, Christina got a part on the *Mickey
Mouse Club*, a TV show (4) ....
....
.... She was on it for the next two
years along with two other people who are now
big names – Britney Spears and Justin
Timberlake. While she was on the *Mickey Mouse
Club*, Christina felt very **lonely** at school. 'I
wanted to have friends and be like everyone else,'
she says, 'I wanted to be a normal kid. But
people get jealous of your success and it creates
problems.'

The difficulties made Christina work harder at her
music. She says, 'I think that's why I **focused** on
my career. My dream of becoming a recording
artist helped me.' Christina's **talent** and energy
were recognised by the world very soon. When
she was still only eighteen, (5)..............................
.... *Genie In A Bottle*
came out in 1999. It went to the top and the rest
is history!

Read

1 **Read the article. Where should these phrases go? Write them in the correct spaces.**

- that has made a lot of people famous.
- dreamed of being a star
- she had her first big hit.
- I lost my friends.
- to be on a show.

2 Write T (true) or F (false).

Christina wasn't interested in singing when she was younger. ....F.........

1 When she was a child, her family often moved house. ....

2 She has had the same best friend all her life. ....

3 She was on TV when she was a young child. ....

4 She didn't have many friends at school. ....

5 She became successful when she was still a teenager. ....

3a Match the words to the meanings.

1 [...] celebrity   a) needing a friend
2 [...] mean   b) famous person
3 [...] lonely   c) give all your time and energy
4 [...] focus   d) another word for *unkind*

3b Guess the meanings of these words, then check in a dictionary and write the translation.

1 army ....

2 talent ....

4 Complete the passage with the following phrases:

- couldn't come   • her little brother
- invited someone else   • some videos
- sorry   • spend the night
- the country

Rosie's friend Sophie had agreed to .spend.the.....
.night.. at her house. Sophie said she would bring
(1)......................... . Then Sophie
phoned and said she (2)............................. .
because she had to babysit (3)...........................

....

Rosie got annoyed because Sophie didn't sound very
(4) .... about it.

If Sophie had phoned in the morning, Rosie could have
(5) .... else. Or she could
have gone to (6)........................... with
Georgia.

Write

5 Write about an argument you had with a friend. Use the sentences in Exercise 4 as a model. Start like this.

My friend ....
had agreed to ....

....

....

....

....

....

....

....

....

....

....

....

....

....

....

....

....

....

....

Study tips

6 Your English will improve if you know your mistakes. Write down the three mistakes which you make most often in English. If you aren't sure, ask your teacher.

I forget the –s in the Present simple (he
knows; she says, etc.) ....

....

....

....

....

....

Talk time

1 **Complete the sentences with these phrases.**

- a bit
- at last.
- isn't that
- see if
- something's happened
- straight away

1 Please ring us .... when you arrive.

2 I've got an extra ticket. Let's ....
Jen wants to come.

3 I've had a letter from Sandra ....

4 Look, Tanya, ... David Beckham
in that shop?

5 Why is everyone standing round the gate? I
think ....
in the park.

6 You're looking .... pale. Do you
want to sit down?

2 **Complete the e-mail with these phrases.**

- especially
- I can show you around
- I can't wait!
- I'm looking forward to seeing you
- I hope that's OK

Hi Gary,

My parents will meet you at the airport on Friday morning.

(1).. with you. I can't come because I'll still be
at school. But (2).. London on Saturday
and Sunday. Unfortunately, I've got another two days of school on Monday
and Tuesday and then it's the summer holidays. (3).. .

On Wednesday morning we're driving down to Cornwall for a week. You're
going to love Cornwall (4).. the surfing.
(5).. . again.

Dan

Let's check

Vocabulary check

1 Match the words to the clues.

bus stop	pavement	tower block
cycle lane	roundabout	traffic lights
~~office block~~	signpost	zebra crossing

It's a tall building where people work. .office block.

1 It's a tall building where people live. ....
....

2 Cars don't go on it, but people walk on it.
....

3 You wait here for a bus. ....

4 You cross the road here. ....

5 When they're red, the cars stop. When they're green, the cars go. ....

6 This little road is only for cyclists. ....

7 You'll see a .... that says, To The Zoo.

8 Go around the ...., and take the second exit.

Grammar check

2 Correct the mistake in each sentence.
∧ = there's a word missing; X = change one word; ↪ = change the order of two words; * = you must delete one word.

You told that she couldn't do it. X
You said that she couldn't do it.

1 There weren't any eggs yesterday because Jo has eaten them all. X
....
....

2 He said that he broken it. ∧
....

3 If you'd been there, what you would have done? ↪
....
....

4 He said he will lend me his boots but he didn't. X
....
....

5 They wouldn't have been worried if you would had phoned. *
....
....

3 Choose the correct words for each sentence.

If I ... in a hurry, I'd have gone to the café with them.

A wasn't   B hadn't been   C didn't

1 When you arrived we ... finished eating.

A already   B were already   C had already

2 I stayed in bed until eleven thirty because I ... to bed at three in the morning.

A had gone   B have gone   C go

3 Jo ... him that she was going out.

A said   B told   C is telling

4 If you hadn't left the door open, the parrot ... out.

A didn't get   B wouldn't have got   C wouldn't get

5 Finn said he ... interested in classical music.

A wasn't   B wouldn't   C didn't

6 We couldn't get a room at the hotel because we ... reserved one.

A didn't   B hadn't   C weren't

7 You said you ... write to me.

A are   B would   C will

8 We'd have visited them if we ... their address.

A didn't lose   B haven't lost   C hadn't lost

9 Rachel ... she didn't want to go out.

A says   B told   C said

10 I'd have brought my sports kit if you ... me about the game.

A told   B would tell   C had told

GRAMMAR FILE

Present perfect continuous

Affirmative

I've/You've/We've/They've been working.

He's/She's/It's been working.

Negative

I/We/You/They haven't been working.

He/She/It hasn't been working.

Questions

Have I/you/we/they been working?

Has she/he/it been working?

Short answers

Affirmative	Negative
Yes, I/we/you/they have.	No, I/we/you/they haven't.
Yes, she/he/it has.	No, she/he/it hasn't.

***Wh?* questions**

How long have I/we/they been working?

What have you been doing?

Where has she/he been standing?

Why have you been crying?

Who has he been talking to?

- We use the Present perfect continuous to talk about an action which began in the past and which is still going on now, e.g. *It's been raining for two days. She's been talking for an hour.*

- We often use *how long, since* and *for* with this tense, e.g. *How long have you been waiting? I've been standing here for an hour. I've been waiting for you since three o'clock.*

- We can also use the Present perfect continuous to talk about an action which ended very recently when we can still see the results now, e.g. *Have you been painting your room? You've got white paint in your hair!*

- We form the Present perfect continuous with *have/has been* + present participle (-*ing* form), e.g. *I've been looking for you everywhere.*

Past simple passive

Affirmative
I was taken to the station.
You were taken to the station.
She/He/It was taken to the station.
We were taken to the station.
They were taken to the station.

Negative
I wasn't taken to the airport.
You weren't taken to the airport.
She/He/It wasn't taken to the airport.
We weren't taken to the airport.
They weren't taken to the airport.

Questions
Was I left there?
Were you left there?
Was he/she/it left there?
Were we left there?
Were they left there?

Short answers

Affirmative	Negative
Yes, I was.	No, I wasn't.
Yes, you were.	No, you weren't.
Yes, he/she/it was.	No, he/she/it wasn't.
Yes, we were.	No, we weren't.
Yes, they were.	No, they weren't.

- We often use the passive to stress the action, or the time and place of the action rather than the person who does it, e.g. *Ten people were hurt in the accident. The castle was built in 1266. This gold necklace was found in the sea.*
- To make the Past simple passive, we use the Past simple of the verb *be* (*was/were*) and the past participle of the main verb, e.g. *I was hit by a car but luckily I wasn't hurt. They were all invited to a party at the end of term.*
- If we want to say who does the action, we use *by*, e.g. *The picture was drawn by a girl in my class.*
- We don't need to repeat *was/were* when we give a list of actions in the Past simple passive, e.g. *All the clothes were washed, ironed and put away in the cupboard.*
- The rules for tense changes in reported questions are the same as in reported statements. See page 93.

Reported questions

Direct questions
Maria: 'What are you doing, Jen?'
Andy: 'Are you feeling OK, Jen?'
Maria: 'Does your sister speak Russian, Jen?'
Andy: 'Did you see anyone at the shops, Jen?'
Maria: 'How many emails have you written, Jen?'
Andy: 'Who will be at the party, Jen?'
Maria: 'Can you stay for dinner, Jen?'

Reported questions
Maria asked Jen what she was doing.
Andy asked Jen if she was feeling OK.
Maria asked Jen if her sister spoke Russian.
Andy asked Jen if she had seen anyone at the shops.
Maria asked Jen how many e-mails she had written.
Andy asked Jen who would be at the party.
Maria asked Jen if she could stay for dinner.

- If the direct question starts with a *wh* word, use the same *wh* word in the indirect question, e.g. *'What do you want?' She asked what I wanted.* If the direct question is a *yes/no* question, use it in the indirect question, e.g. *'Are you angry?'* becomes *He asked if I was angry.*
- In reported questions the word order is the same as in affirmative statements, e.g. *'When are you going to leave?'* becomes *She asked when I was going to leave.* NOT: *She asked when was I going to leave.*
- We don't use *do/does* in reported questions, e.g. *'When do you usually get up?'* becomes *They asked me when I usually got up.*

10

We've been waiting here for ages

Vocabulary

1 **Match the words to the numbers.**

pepper	.....15.....
cup	....
dessert spoon	....
fork	....
glass	....
jug	....
knife	....
napkin	....
bowl	....
plate	....
salt	....
saucer	....
side plate	....
soup spoon	....
teaspoon	....

Dialogue work

2 **Write the sentences in the correct order to make dialogues.**

- Sam Forester.
- Can we order some drinks, please?
- Certainly. What would you like?
- We booked a table for four.
- Could we have four glasses of lemonade?
- Fine. This is your table.
- What name, please?
- Yes. I'll get you those now.

- Anything else?
- Are you ready to order now?
- One chicken salad, one hamburger and two pizzas.
- One green salad, then.
- What would you like?
- Yes, please. Can we also have a green salad?
- Yes, I think we are.

Sam We booked a table for four. ....

Waiter ....

Sam ....

Waiter ....

Sam ....

....

Waiter ....

Sam ....

....

Waiter ....

Waiter Are you ready to order now? ....

Sam ....

Waiter ....

Sam ....

....

Waiter ....

Sam ....

....

Waiter ....

104

Grammar practice

3 **Use the verbs to write captions in the Present perfect continuous.**

paint   rain   fight   swim   watch   work   ~~work out~~

He's been working out at the gym.

1 It ....

2 They ....

3 They ....

4 She...

....

5 He ....

6 He ....

We use *for* when we're talking about a period of time.

She's been talking *for* 20 minutes.
We've been living here *for* three months.

We use *since* when we give the beginning of the time.

She's been talking *since* two o'clock.
We've been living here *since* January.

4 Write sentences in the Present perfect continuous with *for* or *since*.

> They're talking on the phone. They started talking an hour ago.
> They've been talking on the phone for an hour.

1 He's doing his homework. He started it at two o'clock.

....
....

2 We're cycling around Europe. We started in June.

....
....

3 They're making a tree house. They started it weeks ago.

....
....

4 I'm writing a play. I started in September.

....
....

5 You're standing on your head. You started twenty minutes ago.

....
....

6 She's sending texts. She started ten minutes ago.

....
....

5 Write the verbs in the Present perfect continuous.

> Mum is in the kitchen. She 's been cooking (cook) since six o'clock this morning!

1 I'm tired because I ....
.... (not sleep) well recently.

2 You look tired. What ....
.... (you do) all day?

3 I .... (write) postcards all afternoon. This is the tenth one!

4 Seth .... (wear) that cowboy hat all day. He looks ridiculous.

5 I can't find my keys. I ....
(look) for them all day.

6 You look red. How long ....
.... (you lie) in the sun?

6 Complete the sentences with a verb in the Past simple passive.

allow	give	tell	~~take~~
make	leave	invite	

> This photo was taken when we were on holiday in Turkey last year.

1 We .... a toothbrush, a comb and some socks on the plane when we went to New York.

2 Simon and Jack .... to Andy's party but they couldn't go.

3 Why are you so late? You ....
to be here by nine.

4 This bracelet .... by a friend who lives in Kenya.

5 This watch .... in our bathroom last weekend. Whose is it?

6 I .... to hold one of the lambs on Eddie's farm. It was so cute.

7 Use the prompts to write questions in the Past simple passive.

> (you / invite) to Anita's last party?
> Were you invited to Anita's last party?

1 Where (the money / find)?

....

2 How many plates (break) at the party?

....
....

3 (*Hamlet* / write) by Shakespeare?

....
....

4 When (the telephone / invent)?

....
....

5 (anyone / hurt) in the accident?

....
....

6 Why (the windows / leave) open?

....
....

8 Write who asked you each question and report the question.

best friend   little sister
mother   ~~doctor~~
Geography teacher   football coach

How did you twist your ankle?

The doctor .... asked me
how I had twisted my ankle. ....

Where is your project?

.... asked me
....

When are you going to empty the bins?

.... asked me
....

Why did you miss football?

.... asked me
....

5 Who did you dance with at the party?

....................................asked me
....
....

6 What have you bought for Dad's birthday?

....................................asked me
....
....

9 Report the questions that you asked each person.

Holly, are you busy?

I asked Holly if she was busy.
....

1 Justin, do you like spicy food?

....
....

2 Julia, can you remember the words of the song?

....
....

3 Liam, will you be ready in an hour?

....
....

4 Emma, have you learnt everything for the test?

....
....

Culture spot
Fish and Chips

When women in poor families started to go out to work in factories 150 years ago, fast food became more and more important. There was no one at home to shop and cook so people had to buy food on the way back from work.

The most popular fast food in the nineteenth century was fried fish with a piece of bread. 'Chipped' potatoes, as they were called in those days, were also sold in the street. But at first, no one thought of selling the fish and chipped potatoes together. Then in the 1860s the first two fish and chips shops were opened, one in the north of England and one in London. Soon there were 'fish 'n' chips' shops everywhere. Today there are around 8,100 fish and chip shops in Britain, and fish and chips are the country's favourite fast food, ahead of hamburgers and pizza.

Fish and chip shops also sell meat pies, fish cakes, sausages, roast chicken pieces, large pickled onions, and drinks. But you don't have to buy fish or anything else with your chips. Lots of people just buy chips. You can buy a large, medium or small portion. It just depends how hungry you are!

Fish and chips are usually eaten with lots of salt and vinegar. You can add the salt and vinegar yourself or let the people who work in the shop do it for you. Mayonnaise, which is eaten with chips in Holland and Belgium, is not popular in Britain. Ketchup is popular but you have to pay extra for it. You can buy your fish and chips 'open' so you can eat them as you walk home. Or you can buy them 'wrapped' to keep them warm until you get home.

1 **Read the texts on both pages and answer the questions.**

1 What was the most popular fast food in the nineteenth century?

....

2 When were the first fish and chips shops opened?

....

3 What's Britain's most popular fast food today?

....

4 What are popular things to put on fish and chips?

....

5 Why do some people buy their fish and chips 'open'? ....

....

6 Name three other things you can buy to eat in a fish and chip shop.

....

108

Miranda

I love fish and chips with loads of salt and vinegar. We have them every Thursday. I go to swimming club on Thursday and when my mum picks me up, she always buys fish and chips at the shop opposite the pool.

I prefer English chips to the French fries you get with burgers. They're less greasy and they've got more flavour. Mum and I don't usually eat the batter on the fish.
We think it's fattening!

Portfolio

3 **Write about you and food.**

1 Who usually cooks in your family?
....

2 What's your favourite food?
....

3 Do you enjoy cooking?
....

4 What can you cook?
....

5 What kind of foreign food is popular in your country?
....

6 Have you got a favourite restaurant? What kind of food can you get there?
....
....

7 What's the most popular fast food in your country?
....

8 Is there any food that you don't like?
....

9 Is anyone in your family vegetarian?
....

10 What's a typical meal in your family?
....
....

Vocabulary

2 **Find the words for:**

1 a creamy sauce made with egg and oil
....

2 a cold tomato sauce ....

3 covered in paper ....

4 pastry with meat inside ....

5 kept in salt water or vinegar ....

6 a quantity of food ....

7 full of oil or fat ....

8 milk and flour mixture that fish is fried in
....

Let's read

Fast food

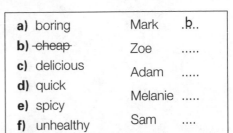

1 **What do five teenagers think of fast food? Read what they say and write the correct letter in each box.**

Mark: It doesn't cost much. That's the main advantage.

Zoe: You never have to wait very long. So it's good if you're in a hurry.

Adam: I love it. I eat it three or four times a week.

Melanie: It's really bad for you. Most of it is really greasy.

Sam: It's always the same. You never get anything new or different.

a) boring	Mark	.b..
b) ~~cheap~~	Zoe	.....
c) delicious	Adam	.....
d) quick	Melanie	.....
e) spicy	Sam	....
f) unhealthy		
g) unusual		

2 **Complete the restaurant advertisement with these words.**

book   courses   delicious   dessert   main   menu   parties   ~~snacks~~   starters   try   types

THE TEXAS BURGER

We are open for meals and ....snacks........... all day.

Our (**1**) .... include soups, salads and seafood.

We serve 20 different (**2**) .... of hamburger.

All (**3**) .... courses come with chips and a salad.

Our most popular (**4**) .... is Sabrina's Chocolate Toffee Cake. Why not come in and (**5**) .... it today.

We also offer 50 different flavours of ice cream.

And they're all (**6**) ....!

We can arrange birthday (**7**) .... but you must

(**8**) .... two weeks in advance. Call us on 028624753.

Try our Sunday lunch (**9**) .... for only £7 for three

(**10**) ....

Let's check

Vocabulary check

1 **The first and last letters are missing from each of these words. They are all things you can see on a dining room table.**

<u>d</u>esser<u>t</u>   <u>s</u>poo<u>n</u>   6   _apki_

1   _nif_   7   _las_

2   _or_   8   _auce_

3   _easpoo_   9   _al_

4   _lat_   10   _eppe_

5   _ow_

Grammar check

2 **Circle the correct words for each sentence.**

These chocolates ... given to me last weekend.

A was   **B** were   **C** aren't

1 I asked him ... happy at his new school.

    A that he was   **B** he was   **C** if he was

2 Cathy asked me if she ... borrow my bike.

    A does   **B** will   **C** could

3 How long ... she been living in Spain?

    A was   **B** did   **C** has

4 Ruth asked me what ... doing at Christmas.

    A I was   **B** will I   **C** I will

5 We ... to the station by coach.

    A took us   **B** were taken   **C** were taking

6 This purse ... found in the school toilets yesterday.

    A was   **B** is   **C** were

7 The cat ... been watching the hamster all day.

    A has   **B** is   **C** was

8 They asked me if I ... like to have lunch with them.

    A did   **B** will   **C** would

9 This cake ... by my sister.

    A was making   **B** was made   **C** were made

10 They ... been eating biscuits all day.

    A have   **B** did   **C** were

Grammar check

3 **Correct the mistake in each sentence.**
∧ = there's a word missing; X = change one word; ↳ = change the order of two words; * = you must delete one word.

How long you been waiting? ∧

How long have you been waiting?

1 I asked him where was he staying. ↳

....

2 She has playing computer games for two hours. ∧

....

....

3 Where was these earrings found? X

....

4 Did you ask him he knew Sandro? ∧

....

5 I was been told to wait here for them. *

....

4 **Make sentences by putting the words in order. Add commas where necessary.**

any / given / lunch / We / weren't

We weren't given any lunch.

1 asked / hadn't / he / him / Mum / phoned / why

....

....

2 been / homework / doing / haven't / I / my

....

3 cushions / garden / in / left / the / these / were / Why / ?

....

....

4 asked / floor / her / I / on / she / sleeping / the / was / why / ?

....

....

Extra!

1 **Read the text and answer the questions.**

The South African swimmer, Natalie Dutoit, has always been a very determined person. When she was a child, she suffered from asthma. Her parents decided that swimming would be good for her health and took her to swimming lessons from the age of six. Natalie didn't like swimming at first. She was frightened of water and held onto the side of the pool. But she wanted to learn to swim and she didn't give up. Bit by bit she became more confident and, by the age of ten, she was breaking all the records for her age group. By the age of fourteen, she was one of South Africa's most promising young swimmers.

But when she was eighteen, Natalie had a serious scooter accident. Her left leg was very badly injured and doctors had to amputate it at the knee. Natalie showed great courage and determination after the accident. Most people take a year to walk with an artificial leg but Natalie practised in the hospital corridor and was walking in five hours. She started swimming again just six weeks after the accident. And just eighteen months after the accident, Natalie took part in the Commonwealth Games at Manchester. She broke two world records and won gold medals in the 50-metre and 100-metre disabled freestyle swimming

events. She also got into the finals of the 800 metre freestyle event for able-bodied swimmers.

Now nineteen-year-old Natalie's goal is to compete against able-bodied swimmers in the next Olympics. 'I'm still the same person and I can reach the same goals,' she says. Natalie, who believes people can learn from every experience in life, says she does get sad sometimes but she doesn't want pity. She says the best thing for her mood is to get into the water. 'I'm not sociable,' she says, 'and in the water I can get away from everyone.'

Natalie is not just a great swimmer. She is also an excellent speaker who fights for the rights of disabled people in South Africa and the rest of the world. She says governments should make it easier for disabled people to study, get jobs and do sport. Her determination to overcome her own problems will certainly give courage to other people.

1 Where does Natalie Dutoit come from?

....

....

2 What was Natalie's problem when she was a child?

....

....

3 At what age did she start going to a swimming pool?

....

....

4 Did she enjoy swimming right from the start?

....

....

5 What happened to Natalie when she was eighteen?

....

....

6 How long after the accident did she start swimming again?

....

....

7 Why did she have to learn to walk again after the accident?

....

....

8 What did she achieve at the Commonwealth Games in Manchester?

....

....

9 What does Natalie want to do in the next Olympics?

....

....

10 What helps Natalie most when she feels sad?

....

....

11 Do you like competitive sports? Why or why not?

....

....

12 What do you think about Natalie Dutoit?
Finish this sentence: **In my opinion, she's**

....

....

2 **Fill the gaps with the correct linking words adding capital letters where necessary.**

and	at first	but	so	when

Natalie Dutoit has always been very determined.
(**1**)........... she was six, her parents decided swimming would be good for her asthma
(**2**)........... she was given lessons. (**3**)...........
she was scared of water (**4**)........... she didn't give up (**5**)........... became one of South Africa's top swimmers.

3 **Put these sentences in the correct order by numbering 1–5.**

a) [...] But she was determined to stay in competitive swimming.

b) [...] At the age of eighteen, Natalie lost her leg in a scooter accident.

c) [...] Only eighteen months after the accident, she competed in the Commonwealth games.

d) [...] She also got into the finals of one event for able-bodied swimmers.

e) [...] She didn't just win medals in the disabled events.

10

Portfolio Dossier

Write a film review for your school magazine. Write around 120 words.

Tips for the task

- First choose the film carefully. Be sure that you have got lots to say about it.

- Give the title and say what kind of film it is. For example, *Harry Potter and the Philosopher's Stone is an exciting action film.*

- Say who the stars are and, if possible, name the director. You can get this information quite easily from the internet. (You should have only used up 30 words by now.)

- Give a simple outline of the story in 30–40 words. Do not go into too much detail. Only say things that you can express in simple English. It is fine to stay in the present tense here. *E.g. Harry Potter's parents are dead. He lives with his horrible aunt, uncle and cousin. His bedroom is a cupboard under the stairs. One day, he gets an invitation to Hogwarts School to study magic. At the school, he makes friends with ….*

- Describe in two or three sentences (30 or 40 words) the scene in the film which you like best. Say why you like it.

You now have 20 or 30 words for the rest.

- Say what you thought about the acting, music, special effects.

- Say what you didn't like about the film.

- Say if you would recommend this film and what age group it is most suitable for.

- Count your words. Make sure you have at least 110 words and no more than 130.

Write your first draft here.

....
....
....
....
....
....
....
....
....
....
....
....
....
....
....
....
....
....
....
....
....
....
....
....
....

- **When you have finished your rough draft, show it to your teacher. She/He will give you feedback by filling in the form on the right.**
- **Your teacher's feedback will help you to improve your first draft.**
- **When you have improved your first draft with the help of the feedback form, write your final version.**

Student portfolio feedback form

Student's name ....

Task ....

Teacher's signature .... **Date** ....

Advice to the student

☐ Your first draft is completely wrong. Start again.

☐ You have not done all of the task. Check the instructions again.

☐ Your work needs to be tidier.

☐ You should add some more ideas.

☐ You should add an introduction.

☐ You should add a conclusion.

☐ You should describe in more detail.

☐ You should give more opinions.

☐ You should use more varied vocabulary.

☐ You shouldn't repeat yourself.

☐ You should check your spelling.

☐ You should check your punctuation.

☐ You need to check your verbs.

☐ You need to check the grammar.

☐ Your handwriting needs to improve.

☐ The style of your language is wrong for this task.

Other comments

....

....

....

....

....

Vocabulary builder

The Vocabulary builder gives you all the words in this book and the Student's Book in alphabetical order. There is also a space for you to write the translation. Each time you learn a new word, write it in your language. In this way you can create your own dictionary.

English	Phonetic	Translation
A		
a bit	/ə ˈbɪt/	
ability	/əˈbɪlɪtɪ/	
able (be able)	/ˈeɪbl/ /biː ˈeɪbl/	
able-bodied	/ˈeɪbl ˌbɒdɪd/	
above	/əˈbʌv/	
accent	/ˈæksənt/	
accept	/əkˈsept/	
access (internet access)	/ˈækses/ /ˈɪntənet ækses/	
accident	/ˈæksɪdənt/	
accommodate	/əˈkɒmədeɪt/	
accommodation	/əˌkɒməˈdeɪʃn/	
ache (I've got stomach ache.)	/eɪk/ /aɪv gɒt ˈstʌmək eɪk/	
achieve	/əˈtʃiːv/	
act	/ækt/	
acting	/ˈæktɪŋ/	
action	/ˈækʃn/	
activity	/ækˈtɪvɪtɪ/	
actor	/ˈæktə(r)/	
actress	/ˈæktrəs/	
actually	/ˈæktʃʊəlɪ/	
admire	/ədˈmaɪə(r)/	
adore	/əˈdɔː(r)/	
adult	/ˈædʌlt/	
adventure	/ədˈventʃə(r)/	
aeroplane	/ˈeərəpleɪn/	
affect	/əˈfekt/	
after	/ˈɑːftə(r)/	
again	/əˈgen/	
against	/əˈgenst/	
ages (for ages)	/ˈeɪdʒɪz/ /fə(r) ˈeɪdʒɪz/	
ago	/əˈgəʊ/	
agree	/əˈgriː/	
ahead of	/əˈhed əv/	
air conditioning	/ˈeə kənˈdɪʃnɪŋ/	
airline	/ˈeəlaɪn/	
airport	/ˈeəpɔːt/	
alcohol	/ˈælkəhɒl/	
allow	/əˈlaʊ/	
almost	/ˈɔːlməʊst/	
alone	/əˈləʊn/	
along with	/əˈlɒŋ wɪð/	
already	/ɔːlˈredɪ/	
altogether	/ˌɔːltəˈgeðə(r)/	
ambulance	/ˈæmbjʊləns/	
amount	/əˈmaʊnt/	
ankle	/ˈæŋkl/	
anybody	/ˈenibɒdɪ/	
anyone	/ˈeniwʌn/	
anyone else	/ˈeniwʌn ˈels/	
anyway	/ˈeniweɪ/	
apart from	/əˈpɑːt frəm/	
appear	/əˈpɪə(r)/	
apply	/əˈplaɪ/	
archaeologist	/ˌɑːkɪˈɒlədʒɪst/	
architect	/ˈɑːkɪtekt/	
Arctic Circle	/ˌɑːktɪk ˈsɜːkl/	
Arm	/ɑːm/	
around (swim around)	/əˈraʊnd/ /swɪm əˈraʊnd/	

English	Phonetic	Translation
around here	/əˈraʊnd hɪə(r)/	
(you aren't from around here)	/juː ɑːnt frəm əˈraʊnd hɪə(r)/	
arrange	/əˈreɪndʒ/	
arrivals	/əˈraɪvlz/	
arrive	/əˈraɪv/	
artist	/ˈɑːtɪst/	
ask	/ɑːsk/	
as soon as	/əz ˈsuːn əz/	
asthma	/ˈæsmə/	
at first	/ət ˈfɜːst/	
at last	/ət ˈlɑːst/	
at least	/ət ˈliːst/	
ate ◄ eat	/eɪt, iːt/	
Atlantic	/ətˈlæntɪk/	
atmosphere	/ˈætməsfɪə/	
attention (centre of attention)	/əˈtenʃn/ /ˈsentə(r) əv əˈtenʃn/	
audience	/ˈɔːdɪəns/	
aunt	/ɑːnt/	
available	/əˈveɪləbl/	
Aztec	/ˈæztek/	
B		
baby	/ˈbeɪbɪ/	
back (adv.)	/bæk/	
back in Manchester	/bæk ɪn ˈmæntʃɪstə(r)/	
back (n.)	/bæk/	
bacon	/ˈbeɪkn/	
baggage reclaim	/ˈbægɪdʒ riːkleɪm/	
baggy	/ˈbægɪ/	
bagpipes	/ˈbægpaɪps/	
balcony	/ˈbælkənɪ/	
ball	/bɔːl/	
ballet	/ˈbæleɪ/	
ban	/bæn/	
banjo	/ˈbændʒəʊ/	
bank	/bæŋk/	
bank manager	/ˈbæŋk mænɪdʒə(r)/	
bar	/bɑː(r)/	
barbecue	/ˈbɑːbəkjuː/	
barn	/bɑːn/	
baseball field	/ˈbeɪsbɔːl fiːld/	
basement	/ˈbeɪsmənt/	
bat	/bæt/	
batter (n)	/ˈbæt (r)/	
battery	/ˈbætərɪ/	
be back by	/biː ˈbæk baɪ/	
bear	/beə(r)/	
became ◄ become	/bɪˈkeɪm/	
because of	/bɪˈkʌz əv/	
been; be; go	/biːn/	
beetle	/ˈbiːtl/	
beginning	/bɪˈgɪnɪŋ/	
bell	/bel/	
belong	/bɪˈlɒŋ/	
beside	/bɪˈsaɪd/	
best (he's doing his best)	/best/ /hiːz duːɪŋ hɪz ˈbest/	
better	/ˈbetə(r)/	
between	/bɪˈtwiːn/	
bird	/bɜːd/	

English	Phonetic	Translation
bit (a bit)	/bɪt/ /ə ˈbɪt/	
bizarre	/bɪˈzɑː(r)/	
bleeding (You're bleeding)	/ˈbliːdɪŋ/ /jɔː ˈbliːdɪŋ/	
blew	/bluː/	
blind (adj)	/blaɪnd/	
blinds	/blaɪndz/	
block of flats	/blɒk əv ˈflæts/	
board	/bɔːd/	
boarder	/ˈbɔːdə(r)/	
boarding school	/ˈbɔːdɪŋ skuːl/	
boat	/bəʊt/	
boil (v.)	/bɔɪl/	
bones	/bəʊnz/	
book	/bʊk/	
boots	/buːts/	
boring	/ˈbɔːrɪŋ/	
born (was born)	/bɔːn/ /wəz ˈbɔːn/	
borrow	/ˈbɒrəʊ/	
both … and	/ˈbəʊθ … ənd/	
bought ◀ buy	/bɔːt, baɪ/	
bowl	/bəʊl/	
bowling (go bowling)	/ˈbəʊlɪŋ/ /gəʊ ˈbəʊlɪŋ/	
boyfriend	/ˈbɔɪfrend/	
branch	/brɑːntʃ/	
break (v.)	/breɪk/	
breathe	/briːð/	
breathing	/ˈbriːðɪŋ/	
bridge	/brɪdʒ/	
bring	/brɪŋ/	
broken ◀ break	/ˈbrəʊkn, breɪk/	
brought ▶		
I've brought a friend along.	/ˌaɪv brɔːt ə ˈfrend əlɒŋ/	
brush	/brʌʃ/	
Brussels	/ˈbrʌsəlz/	
building	/ˈbɪldɪŋ/	
built ◀ build	/bɪlt, bɪld/	
bull	/bʊl/	
burned down	/bɜːnd ˈdaʊn/	
burnt ◀ burn	/bɜːnt, bɜːn/	
bus stop	/ˈbʌs stɒp/	
buy	/baɪ/	
By the way, …	/baɪ ðə ˈweɪ/	

C

English	Phonetic	Translation
cab	/kæb/	
cake	/keɪk/	
call (n.)	/kɔːl/	
call (v.)	/kɔːl/	
came from	/ˈkeɪm frəm/	
canal	/kəˈnæl/	
cancel	/ˈkænsl/	
candle	/ˈkændl/	
cap (baseball cap)	/kæp/ /ˈbeɪsbɔːl kæp/	
captain	/ˈkæptɪn/	
caravan	/ˈkærəvæn/	
career	/kəˈrɪə(r)/	
careful	/ˈkeəfl/	
carpet	/ˈkɑːpɪt/	
carry	/ˈkæri/	
carry on (v.)	/ˌkæri ˈɒn/	
cast	/kɑːst/	
catch	/kætʃ/	
cattery	/ˈkætəri/	
caught ◀ catch	/kɔːt, kætʃ/	

English	Phonetic	Translation
celebrate	/ˈseləbreɪt/	
central heating	/sentrəl ˈhiːtɪŋ/	
central heating control	/sentrəl ˈhiːtɪŋ kəntrəʊl/	
century	/ˈsentʃəri/	
cereal	/ˈsɪəriəl/	
ceremony	/ˈserəməni/	
chain	/tʃeɪn/	
chance	/tʃɑːns/	
chandelier	/ʃændəˈlɪə(r)/	
change	/tʃeɪndʒ/	
chapel	/ˈtʃæpl/	
character (main character)	/ˈkærɪktə(r)/ /meɪn ˈkærɪktə(r)/	
charge (free of charge)	/tʃɑːdʒ/ /friː əv ˈtʃɑːdʒ/	
chase	/tʃeɪs/	
check	/tʃek/	
check in	/tʃek ˈɪn/	
check-in desk	/ˈtʃekɪn desk/	
chef	/ʃef/	
chicken	/ˈtʃɪkɪn/	
Chinese Whispers	/tʃaɪniːz ˈwɪspəz/	
chips	/tʃɪps/	
chocolate (hot chocolate)	/ˈtʃɒklət/ /hɒt ˈtʃɒklət/	
choose	/tʃuːz/	
chores	/tʃɔːz/	
Church of England	/ˌtʃɜːtʃ əv ˈɪŋglənd/	
claws	/klɔːz/	
clean up	/kliːn ˈʌp/	
climb	/klaɪm/	
close to	/ˈkləʊs tə/	
closer	/ˈkləʊsə(r)/	
clothes	/kləʊðz/	
club (golf club)	/klʌb/ /gɒlf klʌb/	
coach	/kəʊtʃ/	
cocoa beans	/ˈkəʊkəʊ biːnz/	
coconut	/ˈkəʊkənʌt/	
coconut palm	/ˈkəʊkənʌt pɑːm/	
coffee bar	/ˈkɒfi bɑː(r)/	
coffee machine	/ˈkɒfi məʃiːn/	
coin	/kɔɪn/	
cold (I've got a cold)	/kəʊld/ /aɪv gɒt ə ˈkəʊld/	
collect	/kəˈlekt/	
colour	/ˈkʌlə(r)/	
colourful	/ˈkʌləfʊl/	
comb	/kəʊm/	
come back	/kʌm ˈbæk/	
come off	/kʌm ˈɒf/	
come on	/kʌm ˈɒn/	
comedy	/ˈkɒmədi/	
communication	/kəmjuːnɪˈkeɪʃn/	
community college	/kəˈmjuːnɪti kɒlɪdʒ/	
competition	/kɒmpəˈtɪʃn/	
competitive	/kəmˈpetɪtɪv/	
complain	/kəmˈpleɪn/	
complete	/kəmˈpliːt/	
complicated	/ˈkɒmplɪkeɪtɪd/	
comprehensive school	/kɒmprɪˈhensɪv skuːl/	
concert	/ˈkɒnsət/	
cone	/kəʊn/	
Congratulations!	/kəngrætʃəˈleɪʃnz/	
container	/kənˈteɪnə(r)/	
conversation	/kɒnvəˈseɪʃn/	
cook	/kʊk/	
cooker	/ˈkʊkə(r)/	
cool	/kuːl/	

English	Phonetic	Translation
corn	/kɔːn/	
cost	/kɒst/	
costume (swimming costume)	/ˈkɒstʃuːm/ /ˈswɪmɪŋ kɒstʃuːm/	
cough (I've got a cough)	/kɒf/ /aɪv ɡɒt ə ˈkɒf/	
could	/kʊd/	
countryside	/ˈkʌntrɪsaɪd/	
courage	/ˈkʌrɪdʒ/	
course	/kɔːs/	
court (basketball/ volleyball/tennis court)	/kɔːt/ /ˈbɑːskɪtbɔːl, vɒlɪbɔːl, tenɪs kɔːt/	
cousin	/ˈkʌzn/	
cover	/ˈkʌvə(r)/	
cow	/kaʊ/	
cowshed	/ˈkaʊʃed/	
cried ◄ cry	/kraɪd, kraɪ/	
criminal	/ˈkrɪmɪnəl/	
criticise	/ˈkrɪtɪsaɪz/	
crocodile	/ˈkrɒkədaɪl/	
crop	/krɒp/	
cross (get cross)	/krɒs/ /ɡet ˈkrɒs/	
crossroads	/ˈkrɒsrəʊdz/	
cruel	/ˈkruːəl/	
crystal	/ˈkrɪstl/	
culture	/ˈkʌltʃə(r)/	
cup	/kʌp/	
curious	/ˈkjʊərɪəs/	
curry	/ˈkʌrɪ/	
cushion	/ˈkʊʃn/	
cut	/kʌt/	
cute	/kjuːt/	
cycle	/ˈsaɪkl/	
cycle lane	/ˈsaɪkl leɪn/	
cyclist	/ˈsaɪklɪst/	

D

English	Phonetic	Translation
dance classes	/ˈdɑːns klɑːsɪz/	
danger	/ˈdeɪndʒə(r)/	
dangerous	/ˈdeɪndʒərəs/	
date	/deɪt/	
daughter	/ˈdɔːtə(r)/	
deaf	/def/	
dear (Oh dear!)	/dɪə(r)/ /əʊ ˈdɪə(r)/	
death	/deθ/	
decent	/ˈdiːsənt/	
decide	/dɪˈsaɪd/	
definitely	/ˈdefɪnɪtlɪ/	
delay	/dɪˈleɪ/	
delicious	/dɪˈlɪʃəs/	
deliver	/dɪˈlɪvə(r)/	
demolish	/dɪˈmɒlɪʃ/	
dentist	/ˈdentɪst/	
departures	/dɪˈpɑːtʃəz/	
deposit	/dɪˈpɒzɪt/	
design	/dɪˈzaɪn/	
dessert spoon	/dɪˈzɜːt spuːn/	
detached	/dɪˈtætʃt/	
determined	/dɪˈtɜːmɪnd/	
dial	/ˈdaɪəl/	
die	/daɪ/	
different	/ˈdɪfrənt/	
directory enquiries	/daɪˌrektrɪ ɪŋˈkwaɪəriːz/	
dirty (get dirty)	/ˈdɜːtɪ/ /ɡet ˈdɜːtɪ/	
disabled	/dɪsˈeɪbld/	

English	Phonetic	Translation
disadvantage	/dɪsədˈvɑːntɪdʒ/	
disappointed	/dɪsəˈpɔɪntɪd/	
disco	/ˈdɪskəʊ/	
discover	/dɪsˈkʌvə(r)/	
disgrace	/dɪsˈɡreɪs/	
disgraceful	/dɪsˈɡreɪsfl/	
dishes	/ˈdɪʃɪz/	
dishwasher	/ˈdɪʃwɒʃə(r)/	
dizzy (I feel dizzy)	/ˈdɪzɪ/ /aɪ fiːl ˈdɪzɪ/	
doctor	/ˈdɒktə(r)/	
dog sledding	/ˈdɒɡ sledɪŋ/	
doll	/dɒl/	
dolphin	/ˈdɒlfɪn/	
done ◄ do	/dʌn, duː/	
donkey	/ˈdɒŋkɪ/	
dorm	/dɔːm/	
double room	/dʌbl ˈruːm/	
doughnut	/ˈdəʊnʌt/	
down (get down)	/daʊn/ /ɡet ˈdaʊn/	
down (just down the road)	/daʊn/ /dʒʌst daʊn ðə ˈrəʊd/	
drama	/ˈdrɑːmə/	
drawing	/ˈdrɔːɪŋ/	
dream		
dresscode	/dres/	
dress	/dres/	
dress rehearsal	/dres rɪˈhɜːsl/	
dressed (get dressed up)	/drest/ /ɡet drest ˈʌp/	
drive	/draɪv/	
duck	/dʌk/	
dump (a bit of a dump)	/dʌmp/ /ə bɪt əv ə ˈdʌmp/	
during	/ˈdjʊərɪŋ/	
DVD player	/diː viː ˈdiː pleɪə(r)/	
dye (v)	/daɪ/	

E

English	Phonetic	Translation
each other	/iːtʃ ˈʌðə(r)/	
early	/ˈɜːlɪ/	
earn	/ɜːn/	
eaten ◄ eat	/ˈiːtn, iːt/	
education	/edʒʊˈkeɪʃn/	
effort	/ˈefət/	
else (anyone else)	/els/ /enɪwʌn ˈels/	
e-mail	/ˈiːmeɪl/	
embarrassing	/ɪmˈbærəsɪŋ/	
emerald	/ˈemərəld/	
emigrate	/ˈemɪɡreɪt/	
encourage	/ɪŋˈkʌrɪdʒ/	
end	/end/	
end of term	/end əv ˈtɜːm/	
engineer	/endʒɪˈnɪə(r)/	
enough	/ɪˈnʌf/	
ensuite	/ɒnˈswiːt/	
entertainment	/entəˈteɪnmənt/	
entirely	/ɪnˈtaɪəlɪ/	
entrance	/ˈentrəns/	
envelope	/ˈenvələʊp/	
equal	/ˈiːkwəl/	
equipment	/ɪˈkwɪpmənt/	
escalator	/ˈeskəleɪtə(r)/	
especially	/ɪˈspeʃlɪ/	
estate (housing estate)	/ɪˈsteɪt/ /ˈhaʊzɪŋ ɪsteɪt/	
European	/jʊərəˈpɪən/	
eve (New Year's Eve)	/iːv/ /njuː jɪəz ˈiːv/	

English	Phonetic	Translation
even (adj.)	/ˈiːvn/	
event	/ɪˈvent/	
ever	/ˈevə(r)/	
everybody	/ˈevrɪbɒdɪ/	
everybody else	/evrɪbɒdɪ ˈels/	
everyone	/ˈevrɪwʌn/	
everything	/ˈevrɪθɪŋ/	
everywhere	/ˈevrɪweə(r)/	
exactly	/ɪgˈzæktlɪ/	
except	/ɪkˈsept/	
exciting	/ɪkˈsaɪtɪŋ/	
exit	/ˈeksɪt/	
expect	/ɪkˈspekt/	
expensive	/ɪkˈspensɪv/	
experiment	/ɪkˈsperɪmənt/	
explain	/ɪkˈspleɪn/	
explore	/ɪkˈsplɔː(r)/	
expression	/ɪkˈspreʃn/	

F

English	Phonetic	Translation
factory	/ˈfæktərɪ/	
fail	/feɪl/	
fair (it's not fair)	/feə(r)/ /ɪts nɒt ˈfeə(r)/	
fairly	/ˈfeəlɪ/	
fairy godmother	/feərɪ ˈgɒdmʌə(r)/	
fallen in	/fɔːln ˈɪn/	
fallen off (fall off)	/fɔːln ˈɒf/	
fame	/feɪm/	
fancy	/ˈfænsɪ/	
fancy dress party	/ˈfænsɪ ˈdres pɑːtɪ/	
fantastic	/fænˈtæstɪk/	
farm	/fɑːm/	
farmer	/ˈfɑːmə(r)/	
farmhouse	/ˈfɑːmhaʊs/	
fashion	/ˈfæʃn/	
faster	/ˈfɑːstə(r)/	
fault (it's my fault)	/fɒlt/ /ɪts ˈmaɪ fɒlt/	
feed	/fiːd/	
feet	/fiːt/	
fell off	/fel ˈɒf/	
fell over	/fel ˈəʊvə(r)/	
fence	/fens/	
ferry	/ˈferɪ/	
festival	/ˈfestɪvl/	
few (a few)	/fjuː/ /ə ˈfjuː/	
fiddle	/ˈfɪdl/	
field	/fiːld/	
filming	/ˈfɪlmɪŋ/	
final	/ˈfaɪnəl/	
finals	/ˈfaɪnəlz/	
find out	/faɪnd ˈaʊt/	
fine	/faɪn/	
fire	/ˈfaɪə(r)/	
firefighter	/ˈfaɪəfaɪtə(r)/	
first (at first)	/fɜːst/ /ət ˈfɜːst/	
fish	/fɪʃ/	
fish cake	/ˈfɪʃ keɪk/	
fishermen	/ˈfɪʃəmən/	
fit (adj.) (keep fit)	/fɪt/ /kiːp fɪt/	
fit (v.)	/fɪt/	
flag	/flæg/	
flamingo	/fləˈmɪŋgəʊ/	
flavour (n.)	/ˈfleɪvə(r)/	
flight	/flaɪt/	

English	Phonetic	Translation
flight attendant	/ˈflaɪt ətendənt/	
floor	/flɔː(r)/	
flying fish	/ˈflaɪɪŋ ˈfɪʃ/	
folk music	/ˈfəʊk mjuːzɪk/	
follow ▶ And to follow, ...	/ənd tə ˈfɒləʊ .../	
food processor	/ˈfuːd prəʊsesə(r)/	
footpath	/ˈfʊtpɑːθ/	
for ages	/fə(r) ˈeɪdʒɪz/	
foreign	/ˈfɒrɪn/	
fork	/fɔːk/	
forward ▶ I'm looking forward to seeing you.	/aɪm ˌlʊkɪŋ fɔːwəd tə ˈsiːɪŋ juː/	
found ◀ find	/faʊnd, faɪnd/	
foundation stone	/faʊnˈdeɪʃn stəʊn/	
fox	/fɒks/	
free	/friː/	
free of charge	/friː əv ˈtʃɑːdʒ/	
freedom	/ˈfriːdəm/	
freestyle	/ˈfriːstaɪl/	
freezer	/ˈfriːzə(r)/	
fresh	/freʃ/	
fridge	/frɪdʒ/	
fried	/fraɪd/	
friendly	/ˈfrendlɪ/	
friendship	/ˈfrendʃɪp/	
frog	/frɒg/	
front (in front of)	/frʌnt/ /ɪn ˈfrʌnt əv/	
frozen	/ˈfrəʊzn/	
full	/fʊl/	
full-time	/ˈfʊl taɪm/	
funny	/ˈfʌnɪ/	
fur	/fɜː(r)/	
future	/ˈfjuːtʃə(r)/	

G

English	Phonetic	Translation
gallery	/ˈgælərɪ/	
game	/geɪm/	
garage	/ˈgærɑːʒ, ˈgærɪdʒ/	
gate	/geɪt/	
geese	/giːs/	
generally	/ˈdʒenrəlɪ/	
get	/get/	
get attention	/ˌget əˈtenʃn/	
get better	/ˌget ˈbetə(r)/	
get bored of	/ˌget ˈbɔːd əv/	
get close to	/ˌget ˈkləʊs tə/	
get on well	/ˌget ɒn ˈwel/	
get out of	/ˌget ˈaʊt əv/	
get ready	/ˌget ˈredɪ/	
get there	/ˌget ˈðeə(r)/	
ghost	/gəʊst/	
girls'	/gɜːlz/	
give up	/gɪv ˈʌp/	
glacier	/ˈgleɪsɪə(r), ˈglæsɪə(r)/	
glass	/glɑːs/	
Go ahead.	/gəʊ əˈhed/	
go back	/gəʊ ˈbæk/	
goal	/gəʊl/	
goat	/gəʊt/	
goggles (swimming goggles)	/ˈgɒglz/ /ˈswɪmɪŋ gɒglz/	
golf course	/ˈgɒlf kɔːs/	
gone ◀ go	/gɒn/	
Good luck!	/gʊd ˈlʌk/	
goose	/guːs/	

English	Phonetic	Translation
gorilla	/gəˈrɪlə/	
got	/gɒt/	
got to	/ˈgɒt tə/	
grammar school	/ˈgræmə skuːl/	
greasy	/ˈgriːsɪ/	
greenhouse	/ˈgriːnhaus/	
grilled	/grɪld/	
group	/gruːp/	
grow	/grəu/	
grow up	/ˈgrəu ˌʌp/	
Guess what?	/ges ˈwɒt/	
guests	/gests/	
guide (tour guide)	/gaɪd/ /ˈtuə gaɪd/	
gym	/dʒɪm/	

H

English	Phonetic	Translation
had ◄ have	/hæd, hæv/	
hair	/heə(r)/	
hairdresser	/ˈheədresə(r)/	
half-time	/ˈhɑːf ˌtaɪm/	
Hallowe'en	/ˌhæləuˈiːn/	
handwritten	/ˈhændrɪtn/	
Hang on!	/hæŋ ˈɒn/	
hang out with	/hæŋ ˈaut wɪð/	
happen	/ˈhæpn/	
harbour	/ˈhɑːbə(r)/	
hard	/hɑːd/	
hate	/heɪt/	
head	/hed/	
hear	/hɪə(r)/	
hear from	/ˈhɪə frəm/	
heard from	/ˈhɜːd frəm/	
heavy metal	/hevɪ ˈmetl/	
hedge	/hedʒ/	
held (it is held every year)	/held/ /ɪt ɪz held evrɪ ˈjɪə(r)/	
hell	/hel/	
helmet (cycle helmet)	/ˈhelmɪt/ /ˈsaɪkl helmɪt/	
help (I can't help)	/help/ /aɪ kɑːnt ˈhelp/	
hen	/hen/	
hide	/haɪd/	
hill	/hɪl/	
hi fi	/ˈhaɪ faɪ/	
hire	/ˈhaɪə(r)/	
hire out	/haɪə ˈaut/	
hold	/həuld/	
hometown	/ˈhəumtaun/	
honey	/ˈhʌnɪ/	
honour (in honour of)	/ˈɒnə(r)/ /ɪn ˈɒnə(r) əv/	
hope	/həup/	
horse	/hɔːs/	
hot	/hɒt/	
hottest ticket	/ˈhɒtɪst ˈtɪkɪt/	
houseboat	/ˈhausbəut/	
How did it go?	/hau dɪd ɪt ˈgəu/	
huge	/hjuːdʒ/	
hunger	/ˈhʌŋgə(r)/	
hurt	/hɜːt/	
husband	/ˈhʌzbənd/	
hypnotist	/ˈhɪpnətɪst/	

I

English	Phonetic	Translation
I wish I could go	/aɪ ˈwɪʃ aɪ kud gəu/	
I'd like ...	/aɪd laɪk .../	
I hope you don't mind.	/aɪ ˌhəup juː dəunt ˈmaɪnd/	

English	Phonetic	Translation
I'm afraid ...	/aɪm əˈfreɪd .../	
I'm afraid not.	/aɪm əfreɪd ˈnɒt/	
ice	/aɪs/	
ice-skating	/ˈaɪs skeɪtɪŋ/	
ideal	/aɪˈdɪəl/	
ill	/ɪl/	
illness	/ˈɪlnəs/	
immediately	/ɪˈmiːdɪətlɪ/	
Incas	/ˈɪŋkəz/	
included	/ɪŋˈkluːdɪd/	
including	/ɪŋˈkluːdɪŋ/	
independence	/ˌɪndəˈpendəns/	
Indian	/ˈɪndɪən/	
indoor	/ˈɪndɔː(r)/	
information point	/ˌɪnfəˈmeɪʃn pɔɪnt/	
injury	/ˈɪndʒərɪ/	
inside	/ɪnˈsaɪd/	
instance (for instance)	/ˈɪnstəns/	
instinct	/ˈɪnstɪŋkt/	
interested in	/ˈɪntrəstɪd ɪn/	
international code	/ˌɪntəˌnæʃnl ˈkəud/	
interpreter	/ɪnˈtɜːprɪtə(r)/	
into (what are you into?)	/ˈɪntu/ /wɒt ə juː ˈɪntuː/	
introduce	/ˌɪntrəˈdʒuːs/	
invent	/ɪnˈvent/	
inventor	/ɪnˈventə(r)/	
invitation	/ˌɪnvɪˈteɪʃn/	
invite	/ɪnˈvaɪt/	
Ireland	/ˈaɪələnd/	
Irish	/ˈaɪrɪʃ/	
iron	/ˈaɪən/	
isle	/aɪl/	
isn't that ...?	/ˈɪznt ðæt .../	

J

English	Phonetic	Translation
jealous	/ˈdʒeləs/	
jewellery	/ˈdʒuəlrɪ/	
job	/dʒɒb/	
join	/dʒɔɪn/	
join in	/dʒɔɪn ˈɪn/	
joke	/dʒəuk/	
journalist	/ˈdʒɜːnəlɪst/	
journey	/ˈdʒɜːnɪ/	
judo	/ˈdʒuːdəu/	
jug	/dʒʌg/	
jump	/dʒʌmp/	
junior	/ˈdʒuːnɪə(r)/	
just right	/dʒʌst ˈraɪt/	
just to be sure	/ˌdʒʌst tə biː ˈʃuə(r)/	

K

English	Phonetic	Translation
keen	/kiːn/	
keep in touch with	/kiːp ɪn ˈtʌtʃ wɪð/	
keep quiet	/kiːp ˈkwaɪət/	
kennel	/ˈkenl/	
kept	/kept/	
kettle	/ˈketl/	
key	/kiː/	
kick	/kɪk/	
kid	/kɪd/	
kill	/kɪl/	
killer whale	/ˈkɪlə weɪl/	
kilt	/kɪlt/	
kind	/kaɪnd/	

English	Phonetic	Translation
...of	/ˈkaɪnd əv/	
...ing	/kɪŋ/	
...it	/kɪt/	
kitchen	/ˈkɪtʃɪn/	
kitten	/ˈkɪtn/	
knee	/niː/	
knife	/naɪf/	
knives	/naɪvz/	
knock down	/nɒk ˈdaʊn/	
knock off	/nɒk ˈɒf/	
known ◄ know	/nəʊn, nəʊ/	

L

English	Phonetic	Translation
laboratory	/ləˈbɒrətrɪ/	
lads	/lædz/	
lady	/ˈleɪdɪ/	
lagoon	/ləˈguːn/	
laid	/leɪd/	
lake	/leɪk/	
lamb	/læm/	
lamp post	/ˈlæmp pəʊst/	
land	/lænd/	
landscape	/ˈlænskeɪp/	
language	/ˈlæŋgwɪdʒ/	
last	/lɑːst/	
last (at last)	/lɑːst/ /ət ˈlɑːst/	
laugh	/lɑːf/	
lazy	/ˈleɪzɪ/	
leave a message	/liːv ə ˈmesɪdʒ/	
left	/left/	
left (if there's any left)	/left/ /ɪf ðeəz enɪ ˈleft/	
leg	/leg/	
lessons	/ˈlesnz/	
Let's get started.	/lets get ˈstɑːtɪd/	
liberty	/ˈlɪbətɪ/	
library	/ˈlaɪbrərɪ/	
lie	/laɪ/	
lie down	/laɪ ˈdaʊn/	
life	/laɪf/	
lifeguard	/ˈlaɪfgɑːd/	
lifetime (of a lifetime)	/ˈlaɪftaɪm/ /ɒv ə ˈlaɪftaɪm/	
light (at first light)	/laɪt/ /ət fɜːst ˈlaɪt/	
lights (street lights)	/laɪts/ /ˈstriːt laɪts/	
like (prep.)	/laɪk/	
limping	/ˈlɪmpɪŋ/	
lines	/laɪnz/	
lit	/lɪt/	
live	/lɪv/	
lively	/ˈlaɪvlɪ/	
living area	/ˈlɪvɪŋ eərɪə/	
loads of	/ˈləʊdz əv/	
local	/ˈləʊkl/	
location	/ləʊˈkeɪʃn/	
lock	/lɒk/	
loneliness	/ˈləʊnlɪnəs/	
long (adj.)	/lɒŋ/	
long (adv.)	/lɒŋ/	
look after	/lʊk ˈɑːftə(r)/	
look for	/lʊk fə/	
look forward to	/lʊk ˈfɔːwəd tə/	
look like	/lʊk laɪk/	
look (n.) (have a look)	/lʊk/ /hæv ə ˈlʊk/	
look (v.)	/lʊk/	
lorry	/ˈlɒrɪ/	

English	Phonetic	Translation
lorry driver	/ˈlɒrɪ draɪvə(r)/	
lost ► lose	/lɒst, luːz/	
lot (one lot of)	/lɒt/	
You only get one lot of parents!	/juː ˌəʊnlɪ get ˈwʌn lɒt əv peərənts/	
lottery	/ˈlɒtərɪ/	
love from	/ˈlʌv frəm/	
love (n.) (fall in love)	/lʌv/ /fɔːl ɪn ˈlʌv/	
loyal	/ˈlɔɪəl/	
luckily	/ˈlʌkɪlɪ/	
luggage (hand luggage)	/ˈlʌgɪdʒ/	
lunch	/lʌntʃ/	

M

English	Phonetic	Translation
machine	/məˈʃiːn/	
made up with	/meɪd ˈʌp wɪð/	
magic	/ˈmædʒɪk/	
mainly	/ˈmeɪnlɪ/	
maize	/meɪz/	
make friends	/meɪk ˈfrendz/	
make people laugh	/meɪk piːpl ˈlɑːf/	
mammal	/ˈmæml/	
manage	/ˈmænɪdʒ/	
manager	/ˈmænɪdʒə(r)/	
marks (get good marks)	/mɑːks/ /get gʊd ˈmɑːks/	
marry	/ˈmærɪ/	
match	/mætʃ/	
mate	/meɪt/	
May I ...?	/meɪ aɪ .../	
maybe	/ˈmeɪbɪ/	
meal	/miːl/	
mean	/miːn/	
meat	/miːt/	
medicine	/ˈmedɪsən/	
meet	/miːt/	
melon	/ˈmelən/	
melt	/melt/	
member	/ˈmembə(r)/	
mention	/ˈmentʃən/	
message	/ˈmesɪdʒ/	
met	/met/	
metal	/ˈmetl/	
method	/ˈmeθəd/	
microwave	/ˈmaɪkrəʊweɪv/	
Middle East	/mɪdl ˈiːst/	
midnight	/ˈmɪdnaɪt/	
miles	/maɪlz/	
milk	/mɪlk/	
miniature	/ˈmɪnətʃə(r)/	
mind	/maɪnd/	
mind ► Do you mind if ...?	/duː juː ˈmaɪnd ɪf.../	
mind (never)	/maɪnd/ /ˈnevə(r)/	
miss	/mɪs/	
mixed	/mɪkst/	
mixture	/ˈmɪkstʃə(r)/	
mobile phone	/məʊbaɪl ˈfəʊn/	
money	/ˈmʌnɪ/	
more	/mɔː(r)/	
motivate	/ˈməʊtɪveɪt/	
motorbike	/ˈməʊtəbaɪk/	
mountain biking	/ˈmaʊntɪn baɪkɪŋ/	
mouse	/maʊs/	
mouth	/maʊθ/	
move	/muːv/	

English	Phonetic	Translation
move in	/muːv ˈɪn/	
much better	/mʌtʃ ˈbetə(r)/	
much later	/mʌtʃ ˈleɪtə(r)/	
muscles	/ˈmʌslz/	
musical	/ˈmjuːzɪkl/	
musician	/mjuˈzɪʃn/	

N

English	Phonetic	Translation
naïve	/naɪˈiːv/	
named after	/ˈneɪmd ɑːftə(r)/	
napkin	/ˈnæpkɪn/	
Naples	/ˈneɪplz/	
native	/ˈneɪtɪv/	
naughty	/ˈnɔːtɪ/	
near	/ˈnɪə(r)/	
nearly	/ˈnɪəlɪ/	
need	/niːd/	
neighbour	/ˈneɪbə(r)/	
neither (neither am I)	/ˈnaɪðə(r)/ /ˌnaɪðə(r) əm ˈaɪ/	
nervous	/ˈnɜːvəs/	
net	/net/	
Never mind.	/nevə ˈmaɪnd/	
new	/njuː/	
newspaper	/ˈnjuːspeɪpə(r)/	
next	/nekst/	
next to	/ˈneks tə/	
Nice to meet you, too.	/ˌnaɪs tə miːt juː ˈtuː/	
Nice to meet you.	/ˌnaɪs tə ˈmiːt juː/	
nil	/nɪl/	
nobody	/ˈnəʊbɒdɪ/	
nor (nor am I)	/nɔː(r)/ /nɔː(r) əm ˈaɪ/	
normal	/ˈnɔːml/	
Northern Ireland	/nɔːðən ˈaɪələnd/	
Not at all.	/nɒt ət ˈɔːl/	
notice	/ˈnəʊtɪs/	
nowhere	/ˈnəʊweə(r)/	
nuisance (be a nuisance)	/ˈnjuːsəns/ /biː ə ˈnjuːsəns/	
nurse	/nɜːs/	

O

English	Phonetic	Translation
occasion	/əˈkeɪʒn/	
ocean	/ˈəʊʃən/	
odd	/ɒd/	
offer	/ˈɒfə(r)/	
office block	/ˈɒfɪs blɒk/	
often	/ˈɒfn/	
olives	/ˈɒlɪvz/	
once	/wʌns/	
one (the old one)	/wʌn/ /ðiː ˈəʊld wʌn/	
onion	/ˈʌnɪən/	
onto	/ˈɒntuː/	
open	/ˈəʊpn/	
opening	/ˈəʊpnɪŋ/	
opera	/ˈɒpərə/	
orchestra	/ˈɔːkɪstrə/	
original	/əˈrɪdʒɪnəl/	
out (10 out of 10)	/aʊt/ /ten aʊt əv ˈten/	
out of (come out of)	/aʊt əv/ /kʌm ˈaʊt əv/	
out there	/aʊt ˈðeə(r)/	
outdoor	/aʊtdɔː(r)/	
outside (adv.)	/aʊtˈsaɪd/	
outside (prep.)	/aʊtsaɪd/	
oven	/ˈʌvn/	
over (all over the floor)	/ˈəʊvə(r)/ /ɔːl ˈəʊvə ðə ˈflɔː(r)/	

English	Phonetic	Translation
over (be over)	/ˈəʊvə(r)/ /biː ˈəʊvə(r)/	
over (over an hour longer)	/ˈəʊvə(r)/ /ˈəʊvə(r) ən ˈaʊə ˌlɒŋgə(r)/	
overcome	/əʊvəˈkʌm/	
overdone	/əʊvəˈdʌn/	
overlook	/əʊvəˈlʊk/	
own (on your own)	/əʊn/ /ɒn jɔː(r) ˈəʊn/	
own (adj.)	/əʊn/	
own (v.)	/əʊn/	
owner	/ˈəʊnə(r)/	

P

English	Phonetic	Translation
Pacific Ocean	/pəˌsɪfɪk ˈəʊʃn/	
pack	/pæk/	
packing (do your packing)	/ˈpækɪŋ/ /duː jə ˈpækɪŋ/	
pain	/peɪn/	
paint	/peɪnt/	
palace	/ˈpælɪs/	
pale	/peɪl/	
panic ▶ Don't panic!	/dəʊnt ˈpænɪk/	
pantomime	/ˈpæntəmaɪm/	
paradise	/ˈpærədaɪs/	
parent	/ˈpeərənt/	
part	/pɑːt/	
pass	/pɑːs/	
passenger	/ˈpæsɪndʒə(r)/	
passion	/ˈpæʃn/	
passport control	/ˈpɑːspɔːt kəntrəʊl/	
patron saint	/peɪtrən ˈseɪnt/	
pattern	/ˈpætən/	
pavement	/ˈpeɪvmənt/	
pay	/peɪ/	
peaceful	/ˈpiːsfl/	
penalty	/ˈpenəltɪ/	
pen-friend	/ˈpenfrend/	
penny	/ˈpenɪ/	
pepper	/ˈpepə(r)/	
per	/pə(r)/	
perform	/pəˈfɔːm/	
performance	/pəˈfɔːməns/	
perfume	/ˈpɜːfjuːm/	
perhaps	/pəˈhæps/	
phone	/fəʊn/	
phone call	/ˈfəʊn kɔːl/	
photographer	/fəˈtɒgrəfə(r)/	
pickled	/ˈpɪkld/	
picture	/ˈpɪktʃə(r)/	
pie	/paɪ/	
piece	/piːs/	
pig	/pɪg/	
pipes	/paɪps/	
pitch (football pitch)	/pɪtʃ/ /ˈfʊtbɔːl pɪtʃ/	
pity (n)	/ˈpɪtɪ/	
plan (n.) (street plan)	/plæn/ /ˈstriːt plæn/	
plan (v.)	/plæn/	
plane	/pleɪn/	
plant	/plɑːnt/	
plate	/pleɪt/	
play (n.)	/pleɪ/	
play (v.)	/pleɪ/	
players	/ˈpleɪəz/	
pleased	/pliːzd/	
pleases (as it pleases)	/ˈpliːzɪz/ /æz ɪt ˈpliːzɪz/	
plot	/plɒt/	

English	Phonetic	Translation	English	Phonetic	Translation
...n	/pəʊɪm/		rang	/ræŋ/	
...y	/pəʊətrɪ/		range	/reɪndʒ/	
...e	/pəˈliːs/		rather than	/ˈrɑːðə ðən/	
police officer	/pəˈliːs ɒfɪsə(r)/		ready ►Are you ready to order?	/ʌ: juː ˌredɪ tuː ˈɔːdə(r)/	
police station	/pəˈliːs steɪʃn/		real	/riːl/	
polite	/pəˈlaɪt/		realise	/ˈrɪəlaɪz/	
pollution	/pəˈluːʃn/		really	/ˈrɪəlɪ/	
pond	/pɒnd/		reason	/ˈriːzn/	
pony	/ˈpəʊnɪ/		rebuilt	/riːˈbɪlt/	
pool (swimming pool)	/puːl/ /ˈswɪmɪŋ puːl/		receive	/rɪˈsiːv/	
poor	/pʊə(r), pɔː(r)/		recently	/ˈriːsəntlɪ/	
popcorn	/ˈpɒpkɔːn/		receptionist	/rɪˈsepʃnɪst/	
popular	/ˈpɒpjʊlə(r)/		recipe	/ˈresɪpɪ/	
post	/pəʊst/		regional	/ˈriːdʒənl/	
post box	/ˈpəʊst bɒks/		regularly	/ˈregjələlɪ/	
post office	/ˈpəʊst ɒfɪs/		rehearsal	/rɪˈhɜːsl/	
postcard	/ˈpəʊskɑːd/		rehearse	/rɪˈhɜːs/	
postcode	/ˈpəʊskəʊd/		reindeer skin	/ˈreɪndɪə skɪn/	
posters	/ˈpəʊstəz/		relax	/rɪˈlæks/	
potato	/pəˈteɪtəʊ/		rent	/rent/	
practise	/ˈpræktɪs/		reporter	/rɪˈpɔːtə(r)/	
prawn salad	/prɔːn ˈsæləd/		research	/rɪˈsɜːtʃ/	
prefer	/prɪˈfɜː(r)/		respect	/rɪˈspekt/	
present with	/prɪˈzent wɪð/		rest day	/ˈrest deɪ/	
pretend	/prɪˈtend/		revise	/rɪˈvaɪz/	
pretty	/ˈprɪtɪ/		rice	/raɪs/	
priest	/priːst/		rich (the rich)	/rɪtʃ/ /ðə ˈrɪtʃ/	
prince	/prɪns/		ride a horse	/raɪd ə ˈhɔːs/	
Prince Charming	/prɪns ˈtʃɑːmɪŋ/		right (all right)	/raɪt/ /ɔːl ˈraɪt/	
prison	/ˈprɪzn/		right ► Is it all right if ...?	/ɪz ɪt ɔːl raɪt ɪf .../	
private school	/praɪvɪt ˈskuːl/		right ► If that's all right.	/ɪf ˌðæts ɔːl ˈraɪt/	
prize	/praɪz/		rights	/raɪts/	
probably	/ˈprɒbəblɪ/		ring	/rɪŋ/	
produce	/prəˈdʒuːs/		road	/rəʊd/	
professional	/prəˈfeʃnl/		roast	/rəʊst/	
programme	/ˈprəʊgræm/		rock	/rɒk/	
promising	/ˈprɒmɪsɪŋ/		rock musician	/rɒk mjuːˈzɪʃn/	
proper	/ˈprɒpə(r)/		role model	/ˈrəʊl mɒdl/	
proud	/praʊd/		romantic	/rəʊˈmæntɪk/	
PS	/piː ˈes/		round (get friends round)	/raʊnd/ /get ˈfrendz raʊnd/	
publish	/ˈpʌblɪʃ/		roundabout	/ˈraʊndəbaʊt/	
punting	/ˈpʌntɪŋ/		route (n)	/ruːt/	
pupil	/ˈpjuːpəl/		royal	/ˈrɔɪəl/	
puppy	/ˈpʌpɪ/		rubbish	/ˈrʌbɪʃ/	
purse	/pɜːs/		rubbish bin	/ˈrʌbɪʃ bɪn/	
push	/pʊʃ/		rucksack	/ˈrʌksæk/	
			run away	/rʌn əˈweɪ/	
Q					
quality	/ˈkwɒlɪtɪ/		**S**		
quarter finals	/ˈkɔːtə ˈfaɪnlz/		sad	/sæd/	
queen	/kwiːn/		sadness	/ˈsædnəs/	
quicker	/ˈkwɪkə(r)/		safe	/seɪf/	
quite	/kwaɪt/		safety	/ˈseɪftɪ/	
			said ◄ say	/sed/	
R			sail	/seɪl/	
rabbit	/ˈræbɪt/		sail across	/seɪl əˈkrɒs/	
race	/reɪs/		sailing	/ˈseɪlɪŋ/	
racecourse	/ˈreɪskɔːs/		sales assistant	/ˈseɪlz əsɪstənt/	
racing (Formula 1 racing)	/ˈreɪsɪŋ/		salmon	/ˈsæmən/	
racism	/ˈreɪsɪzm/		salt	/sɒlt/	
racket	/ˈrækɪt/		salty	/ˈsɒltɪ/	
radiator	/ˈreɪdɪeɪtə(r)/		same	/seɪm/	
rain	/reɪn/		sang ◄ sing	/sæŋ/	
ran ◄ run	/ræn/				

English	Phonetic	Translation
sauce	/sɔːs/	
saucer	/ˈsɔːsə(r)/	
save	/seɪv/	
saw ◄ see	/sɔː, siː/	
scared	/skeəd/	
scary	/ˈskeərɪ/	
scene	/siːn/	
scenery	/ˈsiːnərɪ/	
scenic	/ˈsiːnɪk/	
scientific	/ˌsaɪənˈtɪfɪk/	
scientist	/ˈsaɪəntɪst/	
scooter	/ˈskuːtə(r)/	
score (n.)	/skɔː(r)/	
score (v.)	/skɔː(r)/	
Scots (the Scots)	/skɒts/ /ðə ˈskɒts/	
Scottish	/ˈskɒtɪʃ/	
scream	/skriːm/	
script	/skrɪpt/	
sea	/siː/	
seal	/siːl/	
seat	/siːt/	
secondary school	/ˈsekəndrɪ skuːl/	
secret	/ˈsiːkrət/	
See if ...	/siː ɪf .../	
See you.	/siː juː/	
See you there.	/siː juː ˈðeə(r)/	
seen ◄ see	/siːn, siː/	
selective	/sɪˈlektɪv/	
semi-detached	/ˌsemi dɪˈtætʃt/	
semi-finals	/ˌsemi ˈfaɪnlz/	
send	/send/	
senior	/ˈsiːnɪə(r)/	
separate	/ˈsepərət/	
series	/ˈsɪəriːz/	
serious (be serious)	/ˈsɪərɪəs/ /biː ˈsɪərɪəs/	
serve	/sɜːv/	
session (training session)	/ˈseʃn/ /ˈtreɪnɪŋ seʃn/	
set (adj.)	/set/	
set (n.)	/set/	
settler	/ˈsetlə(r)/	
several	/ˈsevrəl/	
shake	/ʃeɪk/	
shallow	/ˈʃæləʊ/	
share	/ʃeə(r)/	
shed	/ʃed/	
sheep	/ʃiːp/	
ship	/ʃɪp/	
shirt (football shirt)	/ʃɜːt/ /ˈfʊtbɔːl ʃɜːt/	
shoe	/ʃuː/	
shopping centre	/ˈʃɒpɪŋ sentə(r)/	
shorts	/ʃɔːts/	
should(n't)	/ˈʃʊdnt/	
show (n.)	/ʃəʊ/	
show (v.)	/ʃəʊ/	
show ► We can show you around.	/ˌwiː kən ˈʃəʊ juː əˌraʊnd/	
shower (have a shower)	/ˈʃaʊə(r)/ /hæv ə ˈʃaʊə(r)/	
Shut up!	/ʃʌt ˈʌp/	
Siberian	/saɪˈbɪərɪən/	
sick (I feel sick)	/sɪk/ /aɪ fiːl ˈsɪk/	
side	/saɪd/	
side plate	/ˈsaɪd pleɪt/	
sign	/saɪn/	
sign language	/ˈsaɪn læŋgwɪdʒ/	

English	Phonetic	Translation
signpost	/ˈsaɪnpəʊst/	
simple	/ˈsɪmpl/	
since	/sɪns/	
sincerely (yours sincerely)	/sɪnˈsɪəlɪ/ /jɔːz sɪnˈsɪəlɪ/	
singing	/ˈsɪŋɪŋ/	
single room	/ˈsɪŋgl ˈruːm/	
sink	/sɪŋk/	
size	/saɪz/	
skate	/skeɪt/	
skirt	/skɜːt/	
sleep	/sliːp/	
sleeping bag	/ˈsliːpɪŋ bæg/	
sleepover	/ˈsliːpəʊvə(r)/	
slept ◄ sleep	/slept, sliːp/	
slightly	/ˈslaɪtlɪ/	
slowly	/ˈsləʊlɪ/	
smart	/smɑːt/	
smile	/smaɪl/	
smoking	/ˈsməʊkɪŋ/	
snake	/sneɪk/	
snow	/snəʊ/	
snowboarding	/ˈsnəʊbɔːdɪŋ/	
snowmobiling	/ˈsnəʊməbiːlɪŋ/	
so	/səʊ/	
so (and so on)	/səʊ/ /ənd ˈsəʊ ɒn/	
so (so am I)	/səʊ/ /səʊ əm ˈaɪ/	
soap	/səʊp/	
sofa	/ˈsəʊfə/	
solar-powered	/ˈsəʊlə paʊəd/	
sold ◄ sell	/səʊld, sel/	
solo	/ˈsəʊləʊ/	
solve	/sɒlv/	
somehow	/ˈsʌmhaʊ/	
Something's happened.	/ˈsʌmθɪŋz ˈhæpnd/	
somewhere	/ˈsʌmweə(r)/	
son	/sʌn/	
sonnet	/ˈsɒnɪt/	
soon	/suːn/	
sore (I've got a sore throat)	/sɔː(r)/ /aɪv gɒt ə sɔː ˈθrəʊt/	
sort	/sɔːt/	
sound	/saʊnd/	
soup spoon	/ˈsuːp spuːn/	
south	/saʊθ/	
southern	/ˈsʌðən/	
space	/speɪs/	
spare	/speə(r)/	
spare time	/speə ˈtaɪm/	
speak	/spiːk/	
spend	/spend/	
spicy	/ˈspaɪsɪ/	
spider	/ˈspaɪdə(r)/	
spoken ◄ speak	/ˈspəʊkn, spiːk/	
sportsman	/ˈspɔːtsmən/	
sprained	/spreɪnd/	
spray	/spreɪ/	
squad	/skwɒd/	
stable	/ˈsteɪbl/	
stage	/steɪdʒ/	
stage school	/ˈsteɪdʒ skuːl/	
stall (n)	/stɔːl/	
stamp (v)	/stæmp/	
stand	/stænd/	
stand up	/stænd ˈʌp/	
stand up	/stænd ˈʌp/ /hiː stændz/	

English	Phonetic	Translation
(he stands up for himself)	/ʌp fə hɪmˈself/	
...r (n.)	/stɑː(r)/	
...)	/stɑː(r)/	
...chool	/steɪt skuːl/	
...	/steɪʃn/	
...	/stætʃuː/	
...).)	/steɪ/	
...up	/steɪ ˈʌp/	
...(v.)	/steɪ/	
...with	/steɪ wɪð/	
...ak	/steɪk/	
...k (n)	/stɪk/	
...ck-thin	/stɪk θɪn/	
...ticky toffee pudding	/stɪkɪ tɒfɪ ˈpʊdɪŋ/	
...till	/stɪl/	
...tilts	/stɪlts/	
stir	/stɜː(r)/	
steep	/stiːp/	
stole ◀ steal	/stəʊl/	
stomach	/ˈstʌmək/	
stone	/stəʊn/	
stood	/stʊd/	
stop (bus stop)	/stɒp/ /ˈbʌs stɒp/	
stop it	/stɒp ɪt/	
stored	/stɔːd/	
story	/stɔːrɪ/	
story-telling	/stɔːrɪ telɪŋ/	
straight	/streɪt/	
straight after	/streɪt ˈɑːftə(r)/	
Straight away	/streɪt əˈweɪ/	
stray dog	/streɪ ˈdɒg/	
stream	/striːm/	
street	/striːt/	
streetwise	/striːtwaɪz/	
strict	/strɪkt/	
strong	/strɒŋ/	
struck ◀ strike	/strʌk/	
subject	/ˈsʌbdʒekt/	
suburbs	/ˈsʌbɜːbz/	
successful	/səkˈsesfʊl/	
such as	/ˈsʌtʃ əz/	
suffer	/ˈsʌfər/	
suit (cold-weather suit)	/suːt/ /kəʊld ˈweðə(r) suːt/	
summer	/ˈsʌmə(r)/	
sunk	/sʌŋk/	
sunny (be sunny)	/ˈsʌnɪ/ /biː sʌnɪ/	
superb	/suːˈpɜːb/	
support	/səˈpɔːt/	
sure	/ˈsʊə(r), ʃɔː(r)/	
surf the net	/sɜːf ðə ˈnet/	
Surprise, surprise!	/səˈpraɪz, səˈpraɪz/	
surprising	/səˈpraɪzɪŋ/	
surrounded by	/səˈraʊndɪd baɪ/	
survive	/səˈvaɪv/	
swap	/swɒp/	
sweet	/swiːt/	
swept ◀ sweep	/swept/	
swim	/swɪm/	
swimmer	/ˈswɪmə(r)/	
swimming competition	/ˈswɪmɪŋ kɒmpətɪʃn/	
swum ◀ swim	/swʌm, swɪm/	
syrup	/ˈsɪrəp/	

English	Phonetic	Translation
T		
take	/teɪk/	
take a year out	/teɪk ə jɪə(r) ˈaʊt/	
take an exam	/teɪk ən ɪgˈzæm/	
take home	/teɪk ˈhəʊm/	
take photos	/teɪk ˈfəʊtəʊz/	
talented	/ˈtæləntɪd/	
talk	/tɔːk/	
tall	/tɔːl/	
tannoy	/ˈtænɔɪ/	
tap	/tæp/	
tape	/teɪp/	
tasty	/ˈteɪstɪ/	
taught ◀ teach	/tɔːt/	
tax	/tæks/	
taxi	/ˈtæksɪ/	
tea	/tiː/	
team	/tiːm/	
teapot	/ˈtiːpɒt/	
teaspoon	/ˈtiːspuːn/	
teeth	/tiːθ/	
tell	/tel/	
temperature	/ˈtemprɪtʃə(r)/	
terminal	/ˈtɜːmɪnl/	
terraced house	/ˈterəst haʊs/	
test	/test/	
text message	/ˈtekst mesɪdʒ/	
that	/ðæt/	
theatre	/ˈθɪətə(r)/	
there	/ðeə(r)/	
thing	/θɪŋ/	
think (I think so)	/θɪŋk, aɪ ˈθɪŋk səʊ/	
think about	/ˈθɪŋk əbaʊt/	
though	/ðəʊ/	
throat	/θrəʊt/	
through	/θruː/	
thrown	/θrəʊn/	
ticket office	/ˈtɪkɪt ɒfɪs/	
tidy	/ˈtaɪdɪ/	
tiger	/ˈtaɪgə(r)/	
time	/taɪm/	
time (for a long time)	/taɪm/ /fə(r) ə ˈlɒŋ taɪm/	
time (have a good/great) time	/taɪm/ /hæv ə ˌgʊd, greɪt ˈtaɪm/	
time (on time)	/taɪm/ /ɒn ˈtaɪm/	
time (three times)	/taɪm/ /θriː taɪmz/	
tinned food	/ˈtɪnd fuːd/	
tiny	/ˈtaɪnɪ/	
tired	/ˈtaɪəd/	
T-junction	/ˈtiː dʒʌŋkʃn/	
toaster	/ˈtəʊstə(r)/	
toe	/təʊ/	
together	/təˈgeðə(r)/	
together with	/təˈgeðə wɪð/	
told	/təʊld/	
tomato	/təˈmɑːtəʊ/	
tomorrow	/təˈmɒrəʊ/	
tonight	/təˈnaɪt/	
tonnes	/tʌnz/	
too	/tuː/	
took ◀ take	/tʊk, teɪk/	
took part	/tʊk ˈpɑːt/	
took place	/tʊk ˈpleɪs/	
tooth	/tuːθ/	

English	Phonetic	Translation
top	/tɒp/	
touch (n.) (keep in touch with)	/tʌtʃ, kiːp ɪn 'tʌtʃ wɪð/	
touch (v.)	/tʌtʃ/	
tough	/tʌf/	
tour	/'tʊə(r)/	
tour (on tour)	/'tʊə(r)/ /ɒn 'tʊə(r)/	
tourist guide	/'tʊərɪst gaɪd/	
tournament	/'tɔːnəmənt/	
towards	/tə'wɔːdz/	
towel	/'taʊəl/	
tower block	/'taʊə blɒk/	
town	/taʊn/	
track (athletics/race)	/træk/ /æθ'letɪks, reɪs/	
tracksuit	/'træksuːt/	
tradition	/trə'dɪʃn/	
traffic	/'træfɪk/	
traffic lights	/'træfɪk laɪts/	
train	/treɪn/	
trainers	/'treɪnəz/	
training	/'treɪnɪŋ/	
translator	/trænz'leɪtə(r)/	
transport	/'trænzpɔːt/	
travel	/'trævl/	
traveller	/'trævlə(r)/	
treat	/triːt/	
tribute	/'trɪbjuːt/	
trick (n)	/trɪk/	
trip	/trɪp/	
tropical	/'trɒpɪkl/	
trousers	/'traʊzəz/	
true (come true)	/truː/ /kʌm 'truː/	
trunks (swimming trunks)	/trʌŋks/ /'swɪmɪŋ trʌŋks/	
try	/traɪ/	
try on	/traɪ 'ɒn/	
tuberculosis	/tjuːbɜːkjʊ'ləʊsɪs/	
turtle	/'tɜːtl/	
tutor	/'tʃuːtə(r)/	
TV presenter	/tiː 'viː prɪˌzentə(r)/	
twin-bedded room	/twɪn bedɪd 'ruːm/	
typical	/'tɪpɪkl/	

U

English	Phonetic	Translation
ugly	/'ʌglɪ/	
Ugly Sister	/ʌglɪ 'sɪstə(r)/	
UK	/juː 'keɪ/	
uncle	/'ʌŋkl/	
under	/'ʌndə(r)/	
under-18 nights	/ʌndə(r) eɪ'tiːn naɪts/	
unfair	/ʌn'feə(r)/	
unfortunately	/ʌn'fɔːtʃənətlɪ/	
unhappy	/ʌn'hæpɪ/	
United Kingdom	/juːnaɪtɪd 'kɪŋdəm/	
unlike	/ʌn'laɪk/	
until	/ən'tɪl/	
unusual	/ʌn'juːʒʊəl/	
up (up and down)	/ʌp/ /ʌp ən 'daʊn/	
upset	/ʌp'set/	
upstairs	/ʌp'steəz/	
USA	/juː es 'eɪ/	
use	/juːz/	

V

English	Phonetic	Translation
valuable	/'væljəbl/	
van	/væn/	

English	Phonetic	Translation
vast	/vɑːst/	
version (rock opera version)	/'vɜːʒn/ /rɒk 'ɒpərə vɜːʒn/	
very	/'verɪ/	
vet	/vet/	
video player	/'vɪdɪəʊ pleɪə(r)/	
view (in our view)	/vjuː/ /ɪn 'aʊə vjuː/	
view (to have a good view of)	/vjuː/ /tə hæv ə gʊd 'vjuːəv/	
village	/'vɪlɪdʒ/	
visit	/'vɪzɪt/	
voluntary work	/'vɒləntrɪ wɜːk/	
volunteer (n.)	/vɒlən'tɪə(r)/	
volunteer (v.)	/vɒlən'tɪə(r)/	

W

English	Phonetic	Translation
waist	/weɪst/	
wait ▶ I can't wait!	/aɪ kɑːnt 'weɪt/	
wait for	/'weɪt fə(r)/	
Wales	/weɪlz/	
walk all the way from ...	/wɔːk ɔːl ðə 'weɪ frəm .../	
wallet	/'wɒlɪt/	
want	/wɒnt/	
warm	/wɔːm/	
was ◀ be	/wɒz, biː/	
washing machine	/'wɒʃɪŋ məʃiːn/	
washing up	/wɒʃɪŋ 'ʌp/	
(do the washing up)	/duː ðə wɒʃɪŋ 'ʌp/	
watch	/wɒtʃ/	
water	/'wɔːtə(r)/	
waterfall	/'wɔːtəfɔːl/	
way	/weɪ/	
way (a long way from)	/weɪ/ /ə 'lɒŋ weɪ frem/	
way (by the way)	/weɪ/ /baɪ ðə 'weɪ/	
way	/weɪ/	
(She was on her way to ...)	/ʃiː wəz ɒn hɜː ˌweɪ tə .../	
wear	/weə(r)/	
web (the web)	/web/ /ðə 'web/	
website	/'websaɪt/	
weigh	/weɪ/	
well	/wel/	
well (as well as)	/wel/ /əz 'wel əz/	
well (as well)	/wel/ /əz 'wel/	
well (do well)	/wel/ /duː 'wel/	
Well done!	/wel 'dʌn/	
Well played!	/wel 'pleɪd/	
Welsh	/welʃ/	
went ◀ go	/went, gəʊ/	
were ◀ be	/wɜː(r), biː/	
wet	/wet/	
What sort of ...?	/'wɒt sɔːt əv .../	
What would you like?	/wɒt wʊd juː 'laɪk/	
wheelies (do wheelies)	/wiːliːz/ /duː wiːliːz/	
while	/waɪl/	
while (for a while)	/waɪl/ /fə(r) ə 'waɪl/	
whistle	/'wɪsl/	
whole	/həʊl/	
wide screen TV	/waɪd skriːn tiːviː/	
wife	/waɪf/	
wild	/waɪld/	
win	/wɪn/	
winner	/'wɪnə(r)/	
wish (make a wish)	/wɪʃ/ /meɪk ə 'wɪʃ/	
without	/wɪð'aʊt/	
wives	/waɪvz/	

English	Phonetic	Translation
ake up ◀ wake up	/wəʊk ˈʌp, weɪk ˈʌp/	
◀ win	/wʌn, wɪn/	
	/wʊd/	
	/wʊdn/	
	/wʊl/	
year	/wɔː(r), weə(r)/	
	/wɜːk/	
t	/wɜːk ˈaʊt/	
Cup	/wɜːld ˈkʌp/	
◀ wear	/wɔːn, weə(r)/	
d	/ˈwʌrɪd/	
▶ Don't worry!	/dəʊnt ˈwʌrɪ/	
uld you like	/ˌwʊd ju: laɪk	
up of tea)?	ə kʌp əv ˈtiː/	
uld you like (a dessert)?	/ˌwʊd ju: laɪk ə dɪˈzɜːt/	
p	/ræp/	
st	/rɪst/	
riter	/ˈraɪtə(r)/	
ritten ◀ write	/ˈrɪtn, raɪt/	
ritten down	/ˈrɪtn ˈdaʊn/	
rong ▶ What's he done wrong?	/wɒts hi: dʌn ˈrɒŋ/	
wrote ◀ write	/rəʊt, raɪt/	
Y		
yacht	/jɒt/	
yard	/jɑːd/	
Yes, please.	/jes, ˈpliːz/	
Yes, that'll be fine.	/jes, ðætl bɪ ˈfaɪn/	
Yes, that's fine.	/jes, ðæts ˈfaɪn/	
yesterday	/ˈjestədeɪ/	
yet	/jet/	
Z		
zebra crossing	/zebrə ˈkrɒsɪŋ/	
zookeeper	/ˈzuːkiːpə(r)/	

Macmillan Education
Between Towns Road, Oxford OX4 3PP
A division of Macmillan Publishers Ltd
Companies and representatives throughout the world

ISBN 1 405 01913 1
ISBN 1 405 07408 6 (with CD Rom)

Designed by Mackerel Design Limited.
Illustrated by Mark Davis.
Cover design by Mark Davis.

The author would like to thank Mark Farrell for his help and support.

The author and publishers would like to thank the following for their kind permission to reproduce photographs:
Alamy/Rubberball p10 Alamy/BananaStock p96 Alamy/Vittorio Sciosia p77 (tl) Digital Vision p108 (tr) Jon Chapple Photography p54 Empics p112 Corbis/Bettmann, p20 (brm) Corbis/Will & Demi McIntyre p43 (tl) Corbis/Ariel Skelley p43, Corbis/Tom Stewart p43 (ml), Corbis/O.Alamany & Vicens p43 (ml), Corbis/Bettmann p68 (cl), Corbis/ Rick Gomez p77 (tl), Corbis/ Macduff/Everton p77 (tl), Corbis/Ric Ergenbright p87 (blm), Corbis Sygma/Graham Tim p87 (br), Corbis/Patrick Ward p87 (br), Corbis/ Vittoriano, Rastelli p88 (br), Corbis Sygma/LA Daily News/Lazar p98, Getty/Photodisc, Image Click/David Hastilow p87 (br), Image Source p62, Photodisc p114, photos for books p11, p32, p44, p65 (bl, ml,) p88 (t) p108 (bl), p109 (tr), Mary Evans Picture Library p20 (bl), Mary Evans Picture Library/ Arthur Rackham p20 (blm).

Picture research by Polkadot Studios, Witney, Oxon.

And a very special thank you to Daniela Morini and Emma Byrne, whose commitment and enthusiasm have contributed so much to this project.

Printed and bound in Spain by Edelvives.
2009   2008   2007   2006   2005
10   9   8   7   6   5   4   3   2   1